Tripping
- OVER -
Presidents

TRIPPING
- OVER -
PRESIDENTS

Best wishes

Matthew Willman

MATTHEW WILLMAN

Reach
PUBLISHERS

Reach
PUBLISHERS

www.matthewwillman.co.za

WORDS OF AFFIRMATION

"Willman brings great enthusiasm to his professional work. He is sensitive to his subjects and understands the ethical issues around being a photographic documenter. He is articulate, diplomatic and with a good sense of humour."

- Oxfam International

"We believe Mr Willman to be a world-class talent, whose striking and evocative images deserve to be exhibited on the world stage."

- Nelson Mandela Foundation

"One really special thing about Matthew ... he's got the bug. He has an absolute sense of overview ... about what is, what went before, and what's to come. Matthew is passionately connected to the complexity of his existence and those around him. I don't want to speak for him; his words and images go beyond what any of us could imagine. I'm sure of Matthew's gift; it's not an issue ... he connects with his passion ... the rest just follows."

- Annie Lennox, musician and songwriter

"Keep smiling all the way, Matthew, as you serve Him to the best of your ability."

- Founding Zambian President, Dr Kenneth Kaunda

"Matthew is a remarkably talented young man and I am thrilled to see the quality of the work he is producing. We have been enriched by many cultures, languages and faiths; it is a heritage in Africa to be shared, experienced and celebrated, as is the diversity of our landscapes, our wildlife, our villages and towns. Thank you Matthew for mediating these to us through your images and stories."

- Archbishop Emeritus Desmond Tutu

"Many photographers entered Nelson Mandela's environment, not necessarily with the aim of just taking a good photo. Matthew was one of the few people who managed to get the most beautiful photographs of Nelson Mandela because he remained focused on his purpose. [it is] a privilege to have worked with Matthew."

**- Zelda la Grange, former personal
assistant to Nelson Mandela**

"Matthew is a professional and highly talented photographer. While being photographed by him I never felt that he was invading my personal space. I appreciate his refreshing approach to his task."

**- FW de Klerk, Former President of the Republic of South
Africa and 1993 Nobel Peace Prize Laureate**

"Meeting honest young people like you makes me feel the struggle was worthwhile. I know now that the freedom we fought so hard for will be protected."

- Winnie Madikizela-Mandela

"Thank you, Matthew, for showing me your work and photographs. I know that every story and every photo is carefully thought out and planned. After all, beauty doesn't just happen."
- Denis Goldberg, Rivonia trialist

"Keep hope alive, Matthew! Continue with dignity."
- Reverend Jesse Jackson, American civil rights activist, Baptist minister, and politician

"I have met with Matthew often to discuss, at length, our South African story. Matthew's desire to increase his knowledge about the struggle for democracy is exemplary for one in his position, for he has nothing to gain but understanding and compassion. I have witnessed the great lengths [he has gone to] and the hardships [he has] endured, in order to capture stories and images. I have no doubt his story will find its place in our collective history."
- Dr Aubrey Mokoape, former leader of the Black Consciousness Movement and Chairman of the Pan Africanist Party, South Africa (PAC)

"Matthew has a wonderful ability to connect with people. He is clearly a person [who is] passionate when it comes to his work and highly skilled in communicating through his words and images."
- Dan Hurley, President, the National Underground Railroad Freedom Center

"You deserve every success nationally and internationally for your outstanding photography and passion for South Africa!"
- Pam Golding, Chairman and founder of Pam Golding Properties

"Matthew Willman is unusual amongst many experienced professional photographers and story tellers. His ability to connect technique and creativity, expression and passion, is undoubtedly a rare gift. Willman is an asset to South Africa and we all could learn more from his determination to be relevant in a changing world."

- Malcolm Lyle, Associate Director of Photography, Durban Institute of Technology

"Mr Willman is a talented journalist who has produced striking and evocative images and stories of Robben Island. His work evokes the power of the human spirit that bears testimony to the history of the struggle for democracy in South Africa. Keep telling your stories."

- Palesa Morudu, Marketing and Communications Manager, Robben Island Museum

"Matthew shows us all that dreams do come true!"

- Pieter Dirk Uys (Evita Bezuidenhout)

"Matthew really does have the Midas touch; great images, great stories. You are a great man, thank you for your hard work."

- Craig David, singer and songwriter

"Matthew's images capture individuals in their unique and special identity, providing uplifting and joy-filled understanding and memories. That's no surprise to anyone who knows Matthew as I do. He has the ability to see and creatively record the essence of life at its best."

- John Pepper, CEO of Proctor & Gamble (retired) and former Chairman of Walt Disney

"Matthews' passion and enthusiasm for his art, his sensitivity and love of people is immediately felt. This is how his magic begins, allowing his vision and mastery to come through his lens. Willman's work is a gift, an artist of world-class standing."

- Monsieur Hubert Guerrand-Hermès, leading member of the House of Hermès International

"Aah yes I must thank Matthew, my cheeky boy."

- Ahmed Kathrada, Former Rivonia trialist, prisoner on Robben Island.

TABLE OF CONTENTS

INTRODUCTION

"There are victories whose glory lies only in the fact that they are known to those that win them."

- Nelson Mandela, Long Walk to Freedom

The heart of a young boy is dangerous; it is volatile, and most of all, it is beautiful. It knows no limitations; it dreams big and falls in love with heroes. Nothing is off limits, everything is an adventure, and running home battered and bruised after a good day out, with big smiles and lots of dramatic stories, reflects a life expressed to the fullest.

I was glad to be home for a bit. Over the past few weeks I had been in New York, working with dancers from across the city, shooting on the streets for a dance project. With bags half unpacked and e-mails begging for my attention, I had nothing more pressing on my mind than to keep a promise I had made to a 14-year-old family member and his best friend, to build a treehouse. At the bottom of my garden, which borders a nature reserve, a tree had grown out through the rocks of the cliff face, with branches two feet thick suspended in space, hovering over the forest below. The tree was begging to become a new place for adventure and imagination. Together we hammered nails, placed planks of wood, laughed and joked non-stop, until our platform, perfectly positioned, was complete.

Many times during the building of that treehouse, I found myself watching these two young chaps make mistakes, assert their authority and crack jokes, whilst all the time living out their fantasies of what they were creating. Often they were clumsy, they didn't follow instructions and many times very nearly found themselves hurtling twenty-five meters down into the ravine below. Fortunately, I had them both secured with climbing ropes so there was no chance of that. Sitting back watching, I knew that there was nothing in my life as a photographer that would mean anything to them. I was important to them not because of my career, but because I gave them the opportunity to have an adventure. They weren't just knocking in nails; they were building a hideout, a place of their own. I gave them a license to dream and an opportunity to feel dangerous. Therein lies the essence of my life. The idea that there exist opportunities to dream, to let our imaginations run free. This is the driving force for so much of my work as a photographer and storyteller today.

It has taken 25 years to compile a collection of stories that allow me to share an insight into some of my adventures and experiences. In truth, the most challenging aspect of writing this book was whether it was good enough to pursue, come what may.

South Africa during the early nineties was in the throes of change. The old apartheid era was shrivelling up fast and new leaders with new ideals were emerging. The importance of building a new constitution and safe-guarding our new-found freedoms were yet to be tested. Back then, we were all riding the wave of hope, smoothing over gaping holes in our society, striving forward to catch up with the rest of the world. Somewhere in the middle of it all was a young boy on the cusp of adulthood, faced with the choice to leave South Africa or to stay and be a part of the change that was happening. I chose to stay and as the age-old saying goes, 'that made all the difference'.

One fateful night, as an idealistic teenager, I made a decision that I would one day shake the hand of Nelson Mandela. Standing in a crowd of thousands, jostling to get a better view of Mr Mandela standing on a podium far away, I knew I had nothing to lose in pursuing that dream.

So many things in life begin as idealistic dreams. Many years ago in South Africa, those who opposed white minority rule drew up a list of ideals that became known as the Freedom Charter. Its vision was lofty. Even today, in post-apartheid South Africa, we strive to achieve what was written 65 years ago. The same can be said for visionary individuals throughout history: Martin Luther King, Mahatma Gandhi, Joan of Arc, and William Wilberforce. Mother Theresa, whilst being questioned by a US Senator in Washington on the impossible enormity of alleviating poverty, politely responded that each one of us is called to be faithful to the task at hand, rather than merely be successful. I didn't know much about Mother Theresa when I met her in 1989, but much of her life and the lives of countless others have been driven by high ideals to change minds and improve lives.

The stories created before, during and after my time with Mandela, although episodic and distinctly removed from each other, are all inter-connected. There is a part of me that exists in 'the bubble', moments I step into and out of my work, and then there's everyday life. When I return home from a trip, the world hasn't changed, no-one is waiting for me at the airport, and I still have to wash the dishes and stand in the queue at the local store for minced meat or a bag of fresh oranges. No-one asks me what happened or tries to soak up this extraordinary adventure. I simply come home with a quiet confidence and go about my life, knowing that there are places out there that I have touched, and appreciating that even if only for a little while, I was a part of it.

This book is a candid account of moments and experiences from my journey. At times, if I have done my job well, the stories will touch on common emotions and feelings that make us all human. My questions are your questions. My naivety and ignorance are the same as yours might be, if you too were to find yourself in any of the situations that I found myself in. What has been written here happened in the midst of everyday life. It highlights moments that show how precious life is and what you can do with it!

I began a journey to meet Nelson Mandela, and in so doing, created a life worth living.

Matthew Willman
Kloof
KwaZulu-Natal, South Africa
May 2017

....

CHAPTER 1

FINDING MANDELA

Sometimes it's not always the realisation of the dream that counts, but the fact that it gave you a life worth living.

I was as nervous as hell. Nine years pursuing every possible avenue to meet Nelson Mandela, and here I was, wondering if I should have worn something a little more casual than the suit and tie I had borrowed. Sitting waiting in that corridor, I had no idea what this defining moment would look or even feel like. I had certainly not imagined anything beyond the moment I would reach out to shake the hand of Mandela.

At the end of the corridor, a woman appeared; there was a light above her head, which gave her quite a commanding appearance, so instinctively I jumped up. The woman didn't wait for me, she indicated for me to come and then slipped through the door behind her.

At the end of the passage was a lounge. Two large sofas with a single, blue wingback chair graced the room, an intimate space I imagined had received many important guests over the years. Soon after 10am, an intimidating bodyguard came through to the lounge; he gave me a quick once over and then moved to the side, slightly out of view.

Even before I saw him, I heard him: that unmistakable voice, a voice I had listened to on television, through the radio and on YouTube for so many years. Zelda la Grange opened the door, and as if God had waved a magic wand, the "Wizard of Oz" himself appeared, exactly as I had imagined him to be for so many years. Of all the people in the world who could possibly walk through that door, it was him, the great man, Tata Mkhulu, Rolihlahla, our President, the visionary, leader, father and inspiration, Nelson Mandela.

I just stood there. I didn't know what to look at first; his white ivory cane, his face, those big hands or his fancy, colourful shirt. I was struggling to accept that Nelson Mandela himself was walking towards me and me alone. I couldn't believe that Nelson Mandela had risen from his chair in his office next door and was walking to come and greet me. Incredible!

I didn't dare move. I had no idea what to do; I literally had no clue what to do next. This person, this myth of a man, was right in front of me, smiling broadly, looking right at me. My whole chest was burning with joy. I could feel every sinew bursting with life and excitement inside of me. Nearly 3 465 days from the day that I stood as a young boy on a street corner in Durban, along with thousands of other people watching Nelson Mandela make a speech some 50 yards away, I finally got to reach out and take hold of his large, welcoming hand. I knew that everything I had done, all the endless hours I had spent hoping and wishing, fighting and reckoning with myself, had reached an end. Finally, the simple dream I had held onto for so long had arrived. I had shared this dream over and over with so many people, some who had supported me and others who had laughed and thought I was stupid. Finally, I was shaking the hand of Nelson Mandela.

The first few moments were filled with a wonderful sense of awe and amazement, until I realised that I had no idea what to do with it all. There I was, finally experiencing the culmination of this long-held dream, with everything going so well, until I suddenly found myself tripping over a tiny stone on the mountain top. What do you do with it, how do you react to those moments after that dream is realised?

I know what I did: I blurted out,

"Good morning, Mr Mandela, Madiba, sir ..." I had no idea what to even call him. Madiba smiled, he nodded. I carried on. "Sir, it has taken me over nine years to shake your hand and meet you, sir."

Madiba gave me a big, engaging smile, his cheeks curving broadly, and in a matter of fact tone he said,

"Ja, and why didn't you just phone me?" In a playful way, his whole face suddenly looked serious, his eyes wide open, fixed on me, expecting an answer.

I was stunned, the three or four people in the room laughed; even Madiba's bodyguard gave a quiet chuckle. Madiba loved it; he continued to hold onto my hand. His other hand leaning on his white ivory cane, he looked around, sharing the moment, smiling and laughing too. It broke the tension and all the anxiety I had felt. What a beautiful moment, what a beautiful, beautiful moment. I can't say it enough. It goes round and round in my head; the day I first met him. It felt like that scene in the film *In Pursuit of Happyness*, where the actor, Will Smith, plays a down-and-out father, who, after years of trying to prove himself, finally gets the nod from the big bosses. He runs out into the street and there's a moment where the camera swirls around him. For the first time, he is able to breathe, he's able to exhale and accept his achievement. He had been released. For those few moments, I felt the same.

I often think *What if I had not doggedly pursued this dream?* It's so daunting and sobering I dare not allow myself to wander down that path too far. When I look at it all in retrospect, I am aware that I was so hell bent on making this dream the centre of my life, that maybe I had missed the bigger picture. Maybe the dream was broader than Mandela. Maybe he was just the catalyst I needed to push me out of my comfort zone, to keep me on the edge, always pushing forward towards something more. As soon as things became too comfortable, I'd instinctively move on. It's as if I needed the tension, the uncertainty and the threat of failure to keep me engaged. It had kept me focused, and that is all that mattered.

I spent one hour with Mandela that morning. I managed to capture some really special images, which would take on a life of their own in the years to come, in ways I'd never thought possible. I guess I simply photographed from the heart, capturing how I saw this man, his humanity.

Later that same day, I returned home, a bit lost. *I had achieved my goal, but now what? What on earth would I do with the rest of my life?* It was not an absurd question to have floating around in my head. Everything up until this point had demanded focus, a certain determination. There was little else in my life I could walk into or create, now that I had met Mandela.

Little did I know that this was not the last and only time I was to spend time with Mandela. Something new was about to be revealed in the weeks and months ahead. The Nelson Mandela

Foundation had begun building what is today The Nelson Mandela Centre of Memory. They needed a photographer to help build an archive of images pertaining to Nelson Mandela's life, as well as the rare opportunity to work privately with Nelson Mandela.

It wasn't immediately after my first encounter with Mandela that things fell into place. That would be way too easy. A few weeks went by before I received the news that maybe there would be another opportunity to photograph Nelson Mandela. It was during my first interaction with the Nelson Mandela Foundation, that I had asked the powers that be if they would consider me working to build a portfolio of images of Nelson Mandela, which the foundation could use as 'memory' images. The idea didn't go down too well at first. Such access was unprecedented, and they certainly did not want another person around Mandela, especially at his advanced age. I would only complicate the delicate balance in place around the great man. This was perhaps why, upon my return, I descended into moments of deep depression. My ego expected acceptance, but reality had proven over and over that I was a very tiny fish in this grand ocean of Mandela's world.

Fridays were usually slow mornings for me. I worked as a waiter on Thursday nights, getting home late, so on Friday mornings I generally slept in. It was perhaps a little after 8:15am. It had been rainy and cold the whole week and this morning was still the same cold, miserable weather. I was awoken by a telephone call. I reached over and whilst still lying in my bed, I answered the call.

There are moments in life you never forget. The person on the other end of the line was calm and told me to sit down. Since I was lying down, I immediately sat up. It seems my boldness to speak my mind that day at the Mandela Foundation had started a chain of events, which culminated in some rational decisions. It turns out I was the perfect candidate to work with the Mandela

Foundation to help build a visual resource of The Mandela Presidential Library, or what is today called The Nelson Mandela Centre of Memory. I was not affiliated with any other organisations. I was independent, showed a keen interest in South Africa's collective history, proven by my work on Robben Island. With all things considered and with utmost caution, it was agreed that there was an opportunity for me to contribute. A door had opened and I was in with a chance.

My role as a commissioned photographer to the Nelson Mandela Foundation would afford me many amazing opportunities to work not only with Nelson Mandela himself, but to have the privilege of photographically documenting various locations across South Africa that pertained to his life. In so doing, I was able to create intimate and celebrated photographic works, telling the story of this remarkable, special man.

I had found purpose!

....

CHAPTER 2

KEEPING THE ENEMY CLOSE

Whatever you do, no matter how crazy or different, just make sure to never lose your dignity.

On the 31st of October 2006, apartheid strongman, the former president of the Republic of South Africa, Mr PW Botha died. A month previously, I had been sitting with him in his lounge, trying not to attack him on a range of issues swirling around in my head. This was not the first time that I found myself in the company of this man, but it was the first time I dared to take out my camera to record a few images of him. Not that it's of any historic importance, but it turns out those few images snapped on that day were the last photos the world would ever see of this iron-fisted, finger-wagging former president.

Two days after Botha died I received a telephone call from his widow, Barbara Botha, asking if I would come down to George to attend the funeral. At first, I was a bit hesitant; in fact, I said no.

Any engagement that I'd had in the past had been in private and part of my journey to Mandela. As I matured, I began to appreciate what this man and the regime behind him had systematically done, especially to the 'non-white' population of South Africa. I was fully engaged, working with the Nelson Mandela Foundation, so why on earth would I go there and be seen burying this hated man? It could potentially derail my career.

After one night of restless sleep, I woke up and called Barbara back to say I would attend. So it was that two days before the funeral, I flew down to George and ended up staying in the Botha's house. I literally walked into a media frenzy of those who hated the man and others who simply couldn't care less. Security was tight, but knowing the former bodyguards, I made my way up the stairs to the front door to greet Barbara and was welcomed in. The house smelt of flowers; every space, including the floor, was taken up with floral arrangements. I had never seen so many proteas in my life.

I noticed that only one of the bouquets was on the floor, a large arrangement of indigenous South African flowers. I asked Barbara who it was from, and she waved her hand dismissively.

"Aah, that's from old 'Kortbroek' (short pants), Marthinus van Schalkwyk."

Politically, it was Marthinus van Schalkwyk who became the last leader of the National Party, and who eventually joined the ANC (African National Congress). The nickname 'short pants' was used to infer his child-like status amongst greater leaders. It was very derogatory, but it clearly showed peoples' dissatisfaction with him. Nevertheless, he too had sent flowers that now graced the floor of the Botha's home.

So, how did I come to find myself in this very strange environment? I certainly did not align myself with the policies of the

National Party government. But there I was, in the thick of things, in PW Botha's house, the day before his funeral. It had all begun one horrible night, camping in the back of my car under a lighthouse at Cape Agulhas.

A cold front weather system had moved in from the South Atlantic and had made landfall around the time I arrived at the southern-most tip of Africa. My plan was to set up camp that night, but with the howling wind and impossible rains, there was no way to pitch a tent. The wind battered my car and the rain was unrelenting. I had spent the past week in Cape Town where, for the first time, I'd had the opportunity to interview Archbishop Desmond Tutu. I realised during my time with 'The Arch' that if I wished to understand apartheid South Africa, the man I really needed to see was the man who had been one of the most formidable presidents of South Africa, PW Botha. I knew he lived in the holiday town of Wilderness, along the Garden Route, east of Cape Town. So, as with many of my ideas, I figured out the basics, left Cape Town and headed east. My night under the lighthouse, cooped up in my car, was spent wrestling with myself. I had no idea what I was getting myself into; waves of fear and intimidation came and went. Just as I had made up my mind to go to find PW Botha, I was gripped with fear again. Throughout the night, I tossed and turned, eventually lying awake, looking out of the back window at the beam of light from the lighthouse above me going round and round.

Mercifully, dawn broke. The rain had abated, but the wind was still causing havoc for anyone who dared to venture out. With a quick breakfast of ProNutro porridge and a comb of the hair, I was off, heading towards Wilderness. If I thought too much about it all, I would drive straight through to Durban without stopping. Being a holiday resort town in the dead of winter, the streets were empty. I pulled up at a filling station to put in petrol and grab something warm to drink. I had no idea where this former president's house was, so I casually went across to a group of black men huddled inside the shop.

"Excuse me, gentlemen, do any of you know where Mnr PW Botha's house is?" I wasn't expecting much by way of reply, but I was wrong.

"Over there." All six of them pointed in the same direction to a red roofed house along what looked like an estuary, facing away from the ocean.

"Thank you." I didn't say anything else; I walked out the shop, climbed in my car and left.

Just off the main freeway and over the train tracks was a small road that was hardly noticeable. It took me down towards the lagoon, sheltered from the pounding waves of the ocean over the rise.

I didn't want to cause any alarm, so I parked my car a little distance from the gates to the house. It was just on 11am. Already the crows in my stomach were battering me about inside. There was a slight drizzle and the clouds hung low. I knew that if I didn't get out and make my move, I would shy away and leave. I grabbed my camera and notebook, climbed out the car and made my way to the front gate. Above the post box was a sign with an anchor on it. Above the anchor were the words, 'Die Anker', which is Afrikaans for 'The Anchor'. The gates were open, which I thought was very strange. There didn't seem to be anybody around, so I walked right in. I was not more than five steps onto the property when a plain-clothed man stepped onto the driveway from behind a clump of bushes. I stopped, allowing him to come to me. The man was obviously some kind of security guard.

"Kan ek jou help?" Great; more Afrikaans. I was useless at

Afrikaans.

I answered in English.

"Hi, yes thanks, my name's Matthew Willman; is this Mr PW Botha's house?"

"Why do you want to know?" he replied in English.

"I've come all the way from Durban, well, actually from Cape Town yesterday, but I'm originally from Durban in KwaZulu-Natal." I was getting myself horribly tongue-tied. "I would like to meet Mr Botha, please."

"I'm afraid he is not in. He has gone to church this morning."

"Oh, umm …" I wasn't too sure what to say next. "Umm, okay, do you perhaps know when he will be back?" I tried to put on my bravest face.

"He's usually back around 11:30am, but he may decide to go for lunch, so I'm not sure. Can I ask you to please leave the property?"

"Of course, yes. Sorry, the gate was open and there wasn't anyone I could see, so I was going to knock on the front door. Thanks for your help; I'll just go and wait in my car up the road."

"You can't wait around. You a security threat. I must ask you to please leave."

Now this chap was beginning to irritate me. Like hell I was going to leave! If anything, he'd spurred me on to get what I wanted.

I mumbled a thank you and left.

Now what do I do? I climbed back into my car and decided to wait. *PW Botha shouldn't be too long. I'd just wait by the gate. Surely he would have to see me then?*

Every 30 minutes or so the security guard would pop his head out from behind his bushes to see if I was still parked a little way up the road. This went on for hours. Every time I spotted him, I'd wave and he'd quickly nip back behind the bushes.

I did leave at one point to find something to eat at the petrol station where I had filled up. I didn't say a word to anyone; I bought the pie and Coke, beat a hasty retreat to my car, jumped in and left. I began to worry that evening was fast approaching: I hadn't seen Mr Botha and I had nowhere to spend the night. The smell in my car was starting to get to me. Usually when I travelled, it was the smell of the odd apple or banana. I became used to it. But on this trip, my car had become a tent on wheels. I also had not showered or bathed in three days, so things were not too kosher. I was hoping that if I did have the opportunity to meet Mr Botha, a quick spray of deodorant would sort me out.

I looked at the clock; it was just after 5pm. I decided I'd wait twenty more minutes and then call it a day, go find a campsite somewhere and give up on this crazy idea.

Not ten minutes had passed when a large, metallic Mercedes Benz E220 rolled past me. All I saw out the corner of my eye as it passed me by was a large figure wearing a hat, sitting in the front passenger seat. As the car pulled into the driveway, I noticed that a lady was driving. She must have been quite short as she appeared to be craning her neck, looking up over the steering wheel.

Immediately, adrenalin kicked in. My heart was thumping. I turned off the radio, grabbed my camera, jacket and notebook, jumped out the car and made a quick step march over to the front gate of the house. The car had parked and I watched as the bodyguard, the same guy who had kept an eye on me for the past seven hours, held open the door of the car whilst keeping a wary eye on me. I was obviously making him feel very uncomfortable.

A large figure emerged from the car. He moved slowly. You could see that he was old, but well enough to do everything on his own. He never once looked up at me, but kept his eyes on the ground. His head nodded as he passed his bodyguard, before making his way up sixteen stairs to the front door of the house. I watched him climb the stairs slowly. At the top, he turned around to look back at his security guard. The guard rushed up the stairs and they spoke. I hadn't waved or said a word. I had just arrived and stood at the front gate.

PW Botha looked up for the first time. Even from the short distance between us, I noticed his eyes flash beneath his hat. He nodded. He took a step back, stood up straight and placed his cane with his two hands resting on it, in front of him.

The guard bounded down the stairs and for the first time acknowledged me with a wave and then a motion that indicated he wanted me to come closer. This was it; I was going to meet the 'Groot Krokodil'.

It was incredibly tense. I walked past the guard; we didn't speak, we both knew what was happening. Only later did I thank him, because he must have had a word with Mr Botha, opening the door to allow me to walk the twenty meters into no-man's land. For all they knew, I could have had a gun under my jacket. I didn't want to turn around; the sight of the guard with his gun at the ready would have completely destroyed any confidence I had.

I remember those stairs, all 16 of them. I didn't look up. I took a brisk jog up to the top and only then did I look up to find myself standing face to face with the man who had become the Prime Minister and then later the President of the Republic of South Africa in the year I was born. It was this man who, in the 1980s, had offered Mandela release, on condition Mandela gave up armed resistance. The finger-wagging, iron-fisted dictator, whose only weakness was his inability to give up power. Instead, he ruled throughout the 1980s, keeping the nation under a State of Emergency due to the violent unrest that was brewing in the townships. The world hated him, but the majority of the Afrikaner volk loved him. He became Minister of Defence before assuming the role of leader of the National Party. He was both a fighter and a reformer. It was PW Botha who, in the mid-1980s, called for a private meeting with Mandela. But it was also PW Botha who entrenched himself as the dominant voice of apartheid rhetoric, only accepting things his way, thus dragging South Africa through many years of civil unrest and a false sense of so-called peace.

I reached out my hand. We greeted.

"Naand, meneer. My naam is Matthew Willman en ek kom van Durban af, en dis 'n plesier …"

(Good evening, sir. My name is Matthew Willman and I come from Durban, and it is a pleasure …)

I had forgotten what 'to meet you' was in Afrikaans. I was devastated. I was coming across so strong, but collapsed into a heap of nerves on the final hurdle. I instinctively looked down.

"Seun, is jy Engels?"

"Ja, meneer." I was still looking down.

"Well then, speak to me in English." Botha's voice was strong; he sounded exactly as I had heard whilst watching documentaries about him. *What the hell was I doing?* I had crossed over to the other side and there was no way to back out without being rude or totally embarrassing myself. My mind was running wild, but I was still holding his hand. They were large hands, with a lot of flesh on them. I was gripping his hand more than he was holding mine. *Gosh, maybe I was the one holding on. Maybe he wanted his hand back.* So I let go. Instead, he held onto my hand.

"Tell me, Matthew," his eyes looking right into the back of my head, "Why do you want to see me?"

Without even thinking, I shot back,

"Well, sir, I believe you are a man who has never wavered in any decision you have made, good or bad. I respect that and wanted to meet you."

Of course, I was sucking up to him, but I wasn't lying to myself in the process. No matter what you think of him, he was a very strong-willed leader, and good or bad, he stuck to his word. I remember Mandela telling us at a later stage that it was easier to fight your enemy when you knew what their boundaries were. When they keep moving the goal posts, then you know you have problems.

PW looked out across the lagoon, away from me for the first time. He let my hand go and whilst turning he said,

"I'm going inside for a cup of tea. Would you like to join me?"

"Yes, sir, thank you, sir, I would."

With that we both went inside.

What was meant to have been only a quick ten-minute meeting turned into a three-day encounter. Yes, that's right, three days. I ended up staying with PW Botha at his house on the lagoon many times over the next six years. That first evening, we talked until past ten o'clock that night. His wife, Barbara Botha, who by that time had fed us dinner and was on her way to bed, asked where I was staying that night.

"I have no idea; I was only meant to have stayed for ten minutes, but we just got talking."

Barbara turned to PW Botha.

"I'm sure he can stay in the spare room?" PW nodded in agreement.

So it was, a night after I had slept in the back seat of my car in the pouring rain under a lighthouse, I found myself sleeping in the guest bedroom of a former president's home, in a room that had well over twenty paintings, sketches and drawings of this man's face, every one of them staring back at me. I dared not keep the light on for too long. I was exhausted and within a few minutes I was fast asleep.

So that's how I came to find myself years later standing amongst hundreds of flowers in the living room of PW Botha's house, the day before his funeral.

The day of the funeral, things went from mildly abnormal to completely unreal. The funeral at the Dutch Reformed Church in the centre of George was scheduled for 11am. At approximately 10am, I was standing around with the family when one of the State Security guards came up to us to tell Barbara that the motorcade was lined up outside, but that they were short of a driver. There was no-one to drive the former president's personal car to the church. When I heard that, I was immediately worried that there wouldn't be space for me in the motorcade.

Barbara Botha swung around; she had an idea.

"Matthew, do you have a driver's licence?"

"Yes, of course."

"Good, you're driving PW's car this morning."

With that, it was settled. I was given the keys and went to find the car.

The motorcade was very intimidating and impressive. I had not anticipated how big a deal this event would be. All morning, there had been threats of sabotage from various factions, so the police were out in full force, ensuring things ran according to plan. I had heard that the State President, Thabo Mbeki, would be in attendance. Helicopters were circling above; huge armoured vehicles protected the front and rear of the twenty car funeral motorcade. Along our flanks, policemen on motorbikes were poised to move. As the motorcade came to life and started to move, police sirens began to blare. Roads were blocked off and as we made our way from the house, along the estuary, turning right on to the N2 highway towards George, I noticed people lining up along the sides of the road to watch as this mass of heavily guarded cars moved past.

Inside my car, I had Barbara's sister and a bodyguard, and right behind the driver's seat was a man, perhaps even more amazed than me to be where he was that day. His name was Leonard.

Leonard was an illegal immigrant, who, for the past few years had been working as PW Botha's 'houseboy' (a domestic worker). He was from the central African nation of Malawi. Leonard couldn't pronounce the letter 'L', so he always introduced himself as 'Renard' and that's what we called him. The sweetest man, he was always happy and did such a wonderful job of cooking, cleaning and making sure that any guest at the house was never without a fresh cup of tea or coffee.

'Renard' and I were in the same boat that day. Never in a million years had either of us thought that we would be driving in PW Botha's funeral motorcade with hundreds of security officers and the country's media focused on us.

The drive to the church took some 30 minutes. As the procession entered the outskirts of George, I noticed large groups of people had gathered and were waving at us. As we arrived in the town, the groups grew larger until there was no walking space on the pavements, only large crowds pressing in. I couldn't tell at first if they wanted to attack us or were simply people from the community who had come out to see this spectacle. When I saw all this, I had an idea.

On the last stretch of road before the church, I looked at 'Renard' in the rear-view mirror and said,

"Renard, can you wind down your window?" He promptly obeyed.

"Renard, I want you to put your hand out the window and

wave."

With a confused look on his face, 'Renard' began to wave in a child-like manner.

I corrected 'Renard' quickly and showed him how an important person must wave.

By this time, the bodyguard in the seat next to me was getting a bit upset. What on earth was I doing? This was a formal occasion, why was this 'houseboy' from Malawi being told to wave?

I looked back in the rear view mirror at 'Renard'. He was confused and was waiting for my further instructions.

"Renard, my dear friend, today you are a president and I am your driver. I want you to wave at your people and make them feel they have connected with you."

With that, 'Renard' in his grey, fake leather suit, leant out of the window and with the gusto and energy that came from the sheer thrill and excitement of the moment, this man, born in a slum on the outskirts of Blantyre in Malawi, who had never gone to school and now found himself driving in a motorcade protected by over 200 South African security police, pretended that he was a president. He waved with all his heart, his smile so broad, I knew, he knew, that this was perhaps the greatest moment of his life. The people on the streets went wild with excitement. They responded by dancing, clapping and singing. They had no idea who he was. All they knew was that he must have been someone important, perhaps even a leader of some kind and there he was giving them all his love back.

Our motorcade entered the church grounds. The cars parked in an orderly fashion. I realised we were parked right next to Barbara. Seeing my blood red eyes and tears, Barbara gave me a massive hug and said,

"I know this is a very sad occasion." She took my hand and

walked with me to the front steps of the church.

The then president of South Africa, Mr Thabo Mbeki, greeted us at the top of the stairs. He gave me a hug and offered me his condolences on the passing of my grandfather. *My what? No, no, no! Everyone had it all wrong!* But it was too late; the church organ began to play and together with former President FW de Klerk, President Thabo Mbeki and a host of dignitaries and important people, I made my way down the central aisle of the church to the front pew to attend the funeral of PW Botha.

I never saw 'Renard' again after that day. Every now and then, when I'm feeling lonely or find myself looking back at these often intense but beautiful moments in life, I think about him. I have no idea what happened to him. *Did he leave South Africa and return to his village in Malawi?* I imagine him sitting in the evenings with his friends and family gathered round a fire outside his hut, regaling them over and over again with the story of how he, for a few moments became the President of Africa!

....

CHAPTER 3

MANDELA'S PRINCE HARRY

Always go out looking your best. You never know what you'll be called.

In the years that Nelson Mandela was alive and well into his retirement, he used the facility of his Foundation to engage with the world, be it publically or in private, when heads of state or influential individuals came knocking. I used to call those years between 2003 and 2011 the cocaine days. The Foundation was buzzing, a hive of activity. There was always an energy about the place. I'd soak it up and feel a part of the team. Members of staff were motivated and purposeful in their work. Those employed at the Mandela Foundation came from a cross-section of our integrated and diverse society. Many times, my experience as a photographer enabled me to be a fly on the wall. I got to watch guests and friends of the Foundation come and go. Everyone who came through those front doors went away feeling as if they had touched some part of Mandela's legacy. It was a very special place and I loved it.

I remember once whilst I was going about my work at the Foundation, one of the staff members approached me and started to laugh. I had no idea what was so funny, which immediately made me nervous.

"Matthew, I do not know anyone else, not even Graça Machel (Mandela's wife), who just comes and goes as they please; you just talk to everyone and go around where you want, from the CEO's office to the rest of us here in administration. Who are you really?"

We laughed. I don't think I even replied. Without waiting for me to explain myself, she had turned and was walking away, still shaking her head, laughing.

Yes, who was I?

As my time and service at the Mandela Foundation developed, I found a space within the Foundation building that became a safe place for me, a place I came to love, a place I enjoyed returning to over and over again. There were many things I sidestepped, of course. I never involved myself in any issues and I made sure to give anyone having a bad day a wide berth! But those words said in jest that morning sat with me for a while. *Who was I?*

Finding acceptance in any environment is never easy. I was a complete outsider to the everyday goings on of the Mandela Foundation. I would get the call to do a shoot and by day's end I was back on a plane or in my car heading back home, some 600km south-east on the coast. I am sure that even today there are staff members at the Mandela Foundation who have no idea that I lived in another city or so far away. A few times, I would wake up at 3am, leave home and six hours later arrive at the Foundation gates in Johannesburg, ready to do a 10 to 20 minute shoot with Nelson Mandela. I would have a cup of tea and then drive back home. I did it gladly, I loved it. I wanted to count, so in my books twelve hours drive back and forth in one day was a very small sacrifice to make. The only problem was that I had to make sure I was out the gates of the Mandela Foundation by 12 noon as that gave me six hours to drive home, change and start my evening shift as a waiter in my home town, working 'til 11pm or later.

The picture I'm painting here is not what you were expecting to read about, I'm sure. The truth is, during those first years, giving all I could to the Mandela Foundation had nothing to do with money. I was there because I had a purpose and a mission to make a contribution. Yes, I was paid, but it was nowhere near what I needed in order to support myself. You are probably wondering why I didn't focus on being a professional photographer and do shoots that would earn money? The simple answer was that I was trying to do just that. When I first began to shoot for the Nelson Mandela Foundation, the news got out and local newspapers printed a few articles. It was exciting at first, but the publicity began to have a negative effect. Whenever I went out to market myself as a commercial photographer, people were wary of asking me to do shoots, because the name Mandela eclipsed my own name, and often made everyone think I'd charge too much for a shoot. It is true; for a long time, my only option was to wait tables; just go and ask at the *Langoustine* restaurant in Pinetown.

I remember a particular occasion in September one year. The offices of the Foundation were buzzing. Nelson Mandela was coming in and was to hold a press conference that day. Many hours before the scheduled start, the press began to arrive. Amongst them were some well-known anti-apartheid photographers, individuals I had grown up admiring for their bravery and commitment to the struggle; Jurgen Schadeberg, Peter Magubane, 'Bra' Alf Khumalo, Louise Gubb, they were all there. They all knew

Mandela and Mandela knew them. I was in my element.

Moments before the press gathering finished, I nipped out and made my way to the exit doors where Mandela's black seven-series BMW was waiting. Mandela emerged from the auditorium and slowly made his way with an important guest towards his car. I deliberately stood still, and from a good spot I fired off a few images. Mandela was perhaps not more than three meters away from me, when he suddenly stopped. He transferred his white ivory cane to his left hand and with his right hand he first gestured to his guest to get his attention, and then with that same hand, he pointed to me.

Everything seemed to stop; even I was confused. I was so careful not to draw any attention to myself and here Mandela was stopping and now pointing his finger at me. Mandela turned to his guest and with a serious face proceeded to speak,

"You see that boy?" Mandela pointed toward me. The guest readily acknowledged he could see me. "You see that boy?" Mandela repeated. "He is my Prince Harry."

My what? I was completely confused. *Had Mandela mistaken me for the real Prince Harry?* I certainly did not have ginger hair or anything near a British accent.

Everyone laughed, but Mandela carried on.

"He is always so smart; I keep thinking he is Prince Harry."

Madiba gave a broad smile and with that he carried on to the waiting car and that was that.

At the time, I had no idea why Madiba had said that. It was totally out of the blue. I knew that I was not allowed to initiate any direct engagement with Mandela during the course of my work, so to have Mandela's public acknowledgment caught everyone off guard, including me. I remember looking for Zelda, petrified I was about to be fired!

I can only ever imagine that the reason why Madiba said those words to everyone that day was because no matter where I was, whether I was in rural Mvezo, Mandela's homestead in Qunu, or at the Nelson Mandela Foundation, I would always wear a suit. I had committed from day one that whenever I had the opportunity to be in his presence, I would wear a suit. It was the only thing I could offer to show my respect for him.

When Mandla Mandela, Nelson Mandela's eldest grandson, was installed as Chief of the Mvezo homestead in the Eastern Cape (Mandela's birthplace), Madiba attended the ceremony. It was a scorching hot day. The wind was kicking up dust that swirled around the marquees set up for the ceremony. Every single person from the surrounding villages came out that day. It was a chaotic scene. Nothing was going right; even the sound system for the speeches didn't work for some reason. It was so noisy that when Madiba stood up to speak no-one heard a word he was saying. I was no more than four meters away, looking up at Mandela, and all I remember is seeing him talking, making very expressive facial movements and his arms and hands gesturing every now and then. Yet nobody that day heard a word of what he said. Mandela was not talking from notes; he was talking freely about the meaning and legacy of his grandson taking over the helm of Mvezo. At least, that's what I imagined he said. I took lovely photos that day but that was it.

Just after 2pm, Mandela and his entourage were leaving. I took a few images of Mandela saying goodbye to the people and greeting local chiefs from the area before making his way to his car. I slipped out of the marquee and ran about a kilometre down the dusty village road to wait for his car to pass. I thought maybe, for archive purposes, I could get a good shot of his motorcade trundling along on the dusty roads back to Qunu, where Mandela was staying.

The heat was unrelenting and the wind didn't give up its torment of flicking dust all over me. But there I was standing out on the dusty road in a black suit and blue tie, my shiny black shoes now covered in reddish-brown dust.

I watched as the motorcade made its way around the hill and rumbled past me, kicking up even more dust. The only memory I have of that experience is looking through the viewfinder on my camera and seeing Mandela sitting in the back seat. Even though the window was tinted, I remember seeing his silhouette in the cool, air-conditioned car. There was a big smile on his face, and as the car came past I still recall Mandela raising his hand to acknowledge and greet me. The motorcade didn't stop. But I noticed that after his car had passed me, it began to speed up. I like to think they were going slowly so that Madiba had time to greet me.

Yet I come back to my original question, *Who am I?*

It wasn't long after Mandela had spoken those words about me that I was back working tables at the Langoustine Restaurant in Pinetown. It had been a particularly long night; the guests that evening had run us ragged. I had served a table of 12 guests and now as the bill was being paid, I was looking forward to a reasonable tip to make it all worth the effort.

The head of the group, a large, burly man called me over. He told me to sit. In his hand he held the very hefty bill. With a straight face, he said he expected me to work harder and that he was only giving me a R10 tip.

I was devastated.

I stood up and politely asked him what he had done that day.

He went on about the shops he owned and the money he was making.

When he was finished, I looked at him and said,

"Sir, today I woke up at 3am, drove to Johannesburg, worked with Nelson Mandela until 11am, then drove home and spent the rest of the evening serving you. You will never experience what I have the privilege of doing."

With that I gave him back his R10 note, took off my apron and walked out of the restaurant, never to waiter again. I had finally discovered who I was, what I was striving for. It took a disgusting, arrogant businessman and the kind words of Nelson Mandela calling me 'Prince Harry' to finally affirm who I was.

··

CHAPTER 4

THE ARCH'S WAY

I used to think that careers grew through big moments; I have learnt that it's the tiny choices and decisions we make in life that echo in eternity.

There is a South African man I have come to love. I certainly don't agree with everything he says or believes, but he has truly become the moral conscience of South Africa.

Archbishop Desmond Tutu is a true hero of mine. My story with him goes back many years. Nothing makes me smile with instant joy more than listening to 'The Arch' speak. It was inevitable in my journey to Mandela that I would end up working and spending some time with this plucky, exuberant individual.

Lavinia Crawford-Brown, like most personal assistants to people in significant positions, knew how to manage those wanting access to the Archbishop. My first interaction with Lavinia came via a letter I had sent to the Archbishop. Like many of the requests

I made to meet with well-known individuals, it was met with a definite 'No.'

This went on for a few months. The Archbishop was too busy, he was away or they could not come up with a good enough reason except to say no. I got it – I was a nobody. I served no purpose that warranted a meeting, so why, in all truth, would they even consider my request, when perhaps more worthy individuals waited.

I don't know what gave me the idea at first, but it seemed to make sense, so I ran with it. First thing one Monday morning, I headed out to our local shopping centre. I had worked tables the night before, so I had some money saved to help set my plan in motion. I walked into a florist's shop and asked how many flowers I could buy for R80. The assistant showed me the bunch and I said,

"That's great, but I need to have them sent to a building in Cape Town." This increased the price to R100. I agreed and the lady handed me a pen and a piece of paper to write down who the flowers were for and what my message was.

I wrote,

Dear Lavinia,

I have been asking for a 10 minute interview with Archbishop Tutu. For the past eight months, you have said No. I have no other way to express to you how important this is for me. Please accept these flowers.

Matthew Willman

I wasn't sure how desperate to make the note sound, so I just scribbled what came to mind, folded the paper and gave it to the shop assistant. I paid and went home to crawl back into bed, perhaps to hide away as I was not too sure what I had just done.

Later that afternoon, I turned on my computer and there in my Inbox was an e-mail from Lavinia.

Dear Matthew,

I received this morning your beautiful bouquet of flowers; they have really brightened up my day. Would next week Thursday at 10am work to schedule you in for a 30 minute meeting with The Arch?

Kind regards,

Lavinia Crawford-Brown.

I sat back and laughed. I wished I had sent those flowers eight months earlier! It would have saved me a whole lot of wasted energy and emotional torment! When I replied saying that I lived in Durban and that I couldn't make the appointed time, Lavinia very kindly gave me a few options to choose from. What I really needed was a few weeks to earn enough money to drive the 1 600km down to Cape Town. I pulled as many shifts as I could and saved a chunk of change. I was sure I had enough and with bags packed, I was off. The open roads and a new adventure awaited, with an ending that I was certain would lead me right to Archbishop Desmond Tutu. No road, no matter how long the drive, ever looked as welcoming!

From the moment we met, I knew I loved the Archbishop. I walked into his office armed with a pen, a few scraps of paper and my camera. I was ready to listen and learn. I'll never forget how Tutu walked up to me and in his immediately recognisable voice, looked up at me and said,

"My name is Bishop Tutu. I have a big nose and I'm stumpy."

I cried out laughing. How cool was this man? He clasped my hand with his two hands and welcomed me into his office. We found some chairs to sit on and the next thirty minutes quite literally changed the way I saw the world. If anything, it reaffirmed my commitment to meet Mandela.

As the two of us floated from one question to the next, I began to go off track and ask questions that had nothing to do with his opinion about our history. It became more about his ability to handle rejection, walking the tight line between anger and forgiveness. As I asked these questions, Tutu became more and more reflective; he began to take his time in answering. I could clearly see how he was exploring these deep questions with both his personal experiences and his theology.

His words were coming from a very deep and considered place. My own inexperience and inability to handle such interviews left me open to teaching and counsel. As we progressed, Archbishop Tutu took a long, hard look at me. He folded his hands in front of his face, almost in a prayer-like reverence, closed his eyes and continued to speak.

"You know, one of my greatest weaknesses, one of my many weaknesses, is that I love to be loved, and to be vilified as a matter of course, was excruciatingly painful. I needed to be strong, and as I grew stronger, I developed a skin like a rhinoceros. Faith is a commitment to believing in the unseen; it's a risk, but I know that it's a risk I would not want to live without."

There was nothing I could add. My interview was done. Tutu had picked up on why I was really there, why I had driven 1 600km to spend thirty minutes with him. I had no capacity to invoke any further comment, no question good enough; I simply sat there. Fortunately, he wasn't finished.

Whilst I was dealing with whatever was going on inside of me, Tutu opened his eyes, sat back and looking right at me, gave me a light-hearted smile and continued.

"You see, I was not always an Anglican. I was born into a Methodist family. I made a decision, one single decision that ultimately changed my life forever. In 1953, the Nationalist government passed their Bantu Education Act into law. There was no way that I could attain the same level of education as my fellow white students. I was forced to accept what I call their 'gutter' education. So, in order to get a better education, I decided to study through the Anglican Church. The church afforded me the opportunity to get a higher education. I fell in love with what I had experienced and became an Anglican priest a few years later. I continued to study and attained various degrees. Did I know back then that I would become this 'public figure,' this man known to be abrasive whilst taking on the government? Certainly not! My point is this: all it took from me was to make one decision, to reject the offering of the then government to accept this Bantu Education. I rejected it and did everything I could to afford myself a better education and a better life. It was that one choice that I made long ago that made all the difference."

We had gone over our scheduled time. I had a sense that the Archbishop was tired. We were done. I had come to hear answers to my questions and instead I was walking away with a complete shift in thinking that whatever is presented to you, be they boundaries, glass ceilings or pre-conceived ideas of what's right for you, it is the silent, hidden thoughts and choices that will define whether you rise up or continue with the status quo.

As the years have gone by, I have enjoyed other special moments with 'The Arch'. He even did a wonderful two-minute video for me when I launched my Arts Trust in South Africa. Of all the interactions between Archbishop Tutu and Nelson Mandela, there was one occasion that stands out for me. During a public speech, Archbishop Tutu was teasing Mandela that he should dress better and making fun of the flowery shirts Mandela wore in his retirement. Everyone laughed, but Mandela had the last laugh. When it was Mandela's turn to speak, he promptly told the audience that he didn't see why he should take advice from a man who wore a pink dress!

....

CHAPTER 5

THE SCARLET CARPET

Great stories often come from simple moments.

Africa is one crazy, heart-wrenching, heart-warming and totally unscripted continent to live in. Working for over 16 years in the aid and development sector in Africa, I've come to appreciate how unforgiving and highly stressful it is to make a living doing what I do. I've often asked friends what they perceive to be the meaning of success. At times, the answer is all about living well, driving nice cars or flying business class. For others, it's making sure they have good holidays, pay all their bills or simply owning their own home. When I go away thinking about their answers, I'm often left confused, even a bit jaded, about my own definition of success.

When I travel in Africa to places that maps don't even record, we often say to the driver,

"Just head out somewhere into that green colour on the map!"

We are never quite sure what we'll find! The situations are often the polar opposite of what is perceived as success in the western world. When I show people how I travel and the appalling conditions we live and work in, I allow others to share with me their thoughts. No planes, hotels, room service or toilets. When I show a photo of a dusty compound surrounded by an eight foot high, ash-brick fence, a couple of old iron beds out in the open, with tatty mattresses, no roof and an ostrich strutting about in the background, people laugh. They laugh because they have no frame of reference to even begin to understand or appreciate what they looking at.

In capturing the images at the very heart of the human condition across Southern and Eastern Africa, the reality of life is somewhat different. HIV and AIDS, malaria, tuberculosis, food security, water security and primary health care are all issues I have had the privilege of witnessing and working with. But don't be fooled; like the meaning of success, the word 'privilege' has many realities too.

Over several centuries, much of Africa was carved up by colonial powers, and huge swathes of land declared protectorates of Britain, Germany, Italy, Portugal, France and Belgium. This Western European influence sought to draw lines on a map, metaphorically building fences, or moving whole communities in or out of 'their' newly-claimed lands. Military power ensured that formal countries were established, flags were planted and impossible laws pronounced.

In Kenya alone, there are over seventy ethnic tribes, while Malawi has eleven main groups and Mozambique has ten major ethnic groups. This is an inconceivable mix of culture, traditions, beliefs and ideologies. Colonialism screwed down the lid on these ethnic groups and, like a pressure cooker, ruled over them for many decades, often with disastrous effects. As nations across Africa liberated themselves during the 1900s, the horrors of tribalism, ethnic cleansing and political war-mongering by often Marxist-, communist- and socialist-backed governments, created dictators who murdered hundreds of thousands of people to ensure dominance of one tribe over another. In many instances, the targeted enemy were the colonialists themselves. For years, local tribes had fought wars amongst themselves. With the onset of colonialism and democracy they were lumped together and told to make peace, when in reality they hated each other. My greatest fear for Africa is of the outcomes not 'if', but 'when' democracy fails. We've seen what happened in Rwanda during the genocide that saw over a million people murdered in three months, at exactly the same time that Nelson Mandela was coming to power in South Africa and doing what Rwanda had failed to achieve – building national unity.

The issues are intensely complex, diverse and confusing. This mess was created over centuries, and it will be many, many more years before any form of stabilised peace can be ensured.

So, whilst all this is happening, I'm out there driving along old, forgotten roads, trying to find nomadic tribes, camels on the horizon or dodging potholes, thorn-bushes and flooded rivers. No two trips are ever the same. Dry seasons bring a desperate need for water, whilst the wet seasons bring health-care issues. I have spent years zig-zagging across this continent, using my photographs to record self-help projects and programmes that are working towards the ideal of 'sustainable development' amongst rural communities. We have learnt much. A most interesting realisation has been that it was us, the aid agencies, who had to reassess how we engaged with communities rather than 'doing' for communities. It's also been a time of positive growth and development for many of these communities, who previously would have come out with a begging bowl. Instead, they now desire the education, tools and equipment to develop themselves and to sustain their own villages. In southern Mozambique, between Mashishi and Xai-Xai, a man dug a twenty kilometre trench from the river to his village, because he was tired of waiting for government to provide water. Today, his whole village lives and thrives because of his one selfless act.

During this time, it was not uncommon that on a Tuesday I could be with Nelson Mandela, doing a private shoot in his lounge in Johannesburg and then the next day be out in Lusikisiki in the Eastern Cape, documenting the failure of government programmes to prevent children dying from falling into pit latrines. My work has involved the constant transcending of impossible divides and experiences.

I am careful not to come across as having a negative outlook, as I am inherently concerned with all things positive. When I photograph, my clients appreciate that I will accentuate the upliftment, possibility and development of communities in need. It is for this reason that I refuse to photograph wars. War reduces mankind to the lowest form of human nature, and I will not give it that space in my life.

But sometimes, whilst out in the field, I get to step out of our time and into a world that is part myth, part reality. There are stories in Africa yet to be told; some involve people quite literally from other worlds.

One afternoon, a small group of us were trundling along the edges of the Aberdare Mountains in West Central Kenya. We were heading back to the town of Nanyuki, at the foot of Mount Kenya, to overnight there before heading up north to Marsabit and Lake Turkana, sometimes called the 'badlands' of Northern Kenya. You have to know your way around there, or else you'll find yourself in serious trouble.

Driving back in the afternoons, we were often quiet, each of us contemplating our own world of thoughts. By that time, the heat of the day was broken and it was often peaceful. I always drove with my window down, allowing the cool air to rush through my hair. I'd take deep breaths, inhaling the smells of village life, grasslands and, if I was lucky, the nostalgic aroma of the sausage tree that gives off a strong vegetable smell that I love. When the days were particularly hot and the issues we were documenting were pretty heavy, I'd always look forward to the drive back to our compound or tents. Life seemed less urgent, less stressful.

If there was someone talking, it was usually me, sitting up front with the driver, asking questions and learning more about local affairs. I found being up front made it easier to get the driver to stop so I could take a few photographs as and when something caught my eye.

On one specific day, the driver looked at his watch and asked if he could take us to see something. I looked back at the group to see if this was okay; we all agreed, so off we went. A few kilometres further along the road, with Mount Kenya rising up right in front of us, the driver turned off the main road onto a narrow, gravel track that wound its way through the bush. The road was relatively good so we weren't grumbling. We came up from a dip, rounded a corner and happened upon what I could only describe as the most out of place, ornate, little church, built right in the middle of the dense, thorny bush. It was perfectly preserved, with a neat, watered lawn all the way around it. It was the most peculiar sight we'd seen the whole week.

I was intrigued. We climbed out of the car and headed for the tiny, low-slung gate. Nailed to a tree just to the left of the gate, was a sign on an old piece of tin bearing the words: St Philip's Church.

We all stared at this tiny chapel in the middle of nowhere. It was beautiful, especially in the late afternoon sunlight filtering sideways between the trees and through the stained glass windows of the chapel. Our driver began to recount a story.

During the afternoon of the 6th of February 1952, the day King George VI died, Princess Elizabeth was coming to terms with the reality that she was now Queen of the entire British Empire. As the eldest daughter and next in line to the throne, her time had come. We all know the story of how one evening she went up a treehouse, fell asleep a princess, and the next morning came down a queen. But what happened immediately after that?

We all peered through the windows of this tiny church, still not piecing together that this church had anything to do with the story our driver was telling us. Whilst listening, I noticed that around the altar there was a perfectly placed, scarlet red carpet in pristine condition. It looked out of place, considering the humble interior of the chapel. Our driver smiled and continued:

"You see, it's very important to understand that it would be another year before Princess Elizabeth would be crowned, back in London. The first step was for her to be anointed by the church as soon as possible. Word got out that the royal party was looking for a church without delay. Someone suggested that they come here to this tiny chapel, which had been built as an Anglican church."

We all just stood there, staring at the driver as the story unfolded.

Princess Elizabeth arrived at this same unimportant, rural community church and supposedly knelt in front of the missionary priest to be anointed Queen of the Empire of Great Britain.

It was hardly believable. *Surely not? Why hadn't I heard of that story before?* I walked away, and whilst studying the beautiful stonework and the ornate front entrance, I could hardly believe how beautiful and poetic that event must have been all those years ago.

Can you imagine the scene? There you are, a seemingly forgotten missionary priest of the Church of England, living on the northern slopes of Mount Kenya, farming, tending to your chickens, going about your priestly duties, and out of the blue, a motorcade of official vehicles and large black limousines pulls up to your tiny parish church in the bush. Out steps Princess Elizabeth and without warning you are told that it is your duty as representative of God on Earth, for Queen and country, to symbolically bless and physically anoint the next Queen of England. Have you any idea how unimaginable that is?

The priest had probably run away from Europe to hide somewhere in deepest, darkest Africa, and out of the blue, on an absolutely normal day, just as he was about to make a cup of tea and have some bread with a smear of jam, the whole British Empire comes knocking on his door, with the instruction to maintain the succession of power!

This extraordinary story goes round and round in my mind. Whether it happened exactly as the driver told it, I will never know. The most important question for me was to know if the story was true. Fortunately, I can confirm what I actually saw. Inside the chapel, I had noticed the scarlet red carpet, totally out of place in a rural African church. I later discovered that it is recorded that after Her Majesty the Queen's coronation in London, she had a piece of her coronation carpet delivered to that tiny church out in Kenya, to be placed in the church as a testimony to what happened that strange day on the 6th of February 1952.

....

CHAPTER 6

ONE LAST REMARK

Sometimes affirmation comes from the
most unlikely of places.

The protocol around Nelson Mandela was designed to limit and ensure that anyone in Mandela's presence understood the rules of engagement. Many of the rules were unwritten, but common sense prevailed at all times. Madiba was in his advanced old age, he moved about slowly and you had to speak loudly to ensure he could hear. More than anything, it was important to respect his space. On the days when I was called upon to do a photo shoot with Madiba, I arrived early to make sure everything was in place before Madiba arrived. Usually, the photo shoots took place in his office, so the first item on my early morning checklist was to check the lighting, establish where best to stand, and then to go about my work unnoticed. When the opportunity came to engage directly with Mandela, I would have to force myself to look directly at him. For some reason, I felt that looking at him directly was in some way disrespectful.

On one occasion, I was with Mandela in his office and Zelda, his personal assistant, was standing at the door talking to someone. I was calculating the exposure on my camera when I happened to look across to Madiba, who was perhaps only a few steps away from me. I had been fiddling with my camera, doing my best not to draw attention to myself. When I glanced across at him, I did a double take: there he was sitting with his legs crossed, quietly observing me. How long had he been staring at me? It was not a quick look, but a long gaze that followed me. I don't know about you, but with nowhere to hide and not wanting to ask him to look at something else, I immediately looked at the ground. I walked over to the corner of the room, assumed my usual place, waiting for the morning event to happen. For quite a while, I stood and waited there, every now and then looking at him and finding him looking back at me. Have you any idea how intimidating that is? After that occasion, I began to be more attentive of watching Madiba. I became fascinated with how he would keenly observe what was going on around him. I noticed that on many occasions, when he was not asked to do anything, or when he was waiting for things to happen, he would sit and watch people. He was very good at observing whoever was in the room. It wasn't a blank look, but a deep observation of whoever was in the room. Sometimes, only his eyes moved, following people. It was as if he was studiously trying to figure out the nature of the person he was studying.

I had been hoping and praying that Zelda would come back into the room to distract him, but she didn't. I was also aware that in my contract it stated that I was not to engage with Mandela unless he first initiated a conversation. At most, I was to greet and to avoid any interaction. I understood this very clearly. I was there to work and not to partake in what he was doing. Every now and then, without warning, Madiba asked me if I was married.

"Mkhulu?" I looked at him, a bit shocked ... "No, Mkhulu, I'm not married."

"And why are you not married?"

"Mkhulu, it's because I work too hard for you!" I smiled, trying to relax.

"No, that is not good," Madiba frowned, "you must get married."

"Yes, Mkhulu."

He was right; I'd love to be married, but finances and the nomadic life I was leading at the time got in the way of making any meaningful effort in a relationship.

This wasn't the first time he caught me off guard. We were with Madiba in his office one morning, waiting for his guest to arrive. Another cameraman was also in the room, a videographer from Sweden, if I remember correctly. I greeted Madiba in my usual way. Madiba would smile, I'd step back and the show would start. Just as I had positioned myself out of the way, Madiba asked me if I knew Mandla Mandela, his eldest grandson. I nodded and said,

"Yes, Mkhulu, I've known Mandla for a few years now," and reminded him that I was there at his installation as Chief of Mveso the previous year.

Madiba thought for a moment and then nodded before asking another question that left me reeling ...

"Where is your business card?" He said this whilst holding his hand out expectantly.

"Mkhulu?" I replied, questioningly. "I don't have a business card. I mean, I do at home, but I didn't think I would ever need one whilst working with you."

Madiba looked disappointed. He frowned and then proceeded

to lecture me.

"Do you know the Chinese? Every time you meet the Chinese, they give you a business card. It is very important to remember a business card." Madiba was wagging his finger at me. "Where is your card?"

I was devastated. Here I was being asked by the great Nelson Mandela for my business card and I didn't even have one. I'd have given him anything, even my car keys, just to say I gave him something, but a business card? I was blown out the water. He was right though; I wasn't there to sip tea and talk about the events of the world, I was there to work. My association with the Mandela Foundation was only ever to work, so why didn't I have a business card? *Aaarggh.* I wanted to kick myself. The rest of that day at the Foundation was a blur. For some reason, the photo shoot that morning had put me in a foul mood.

I drove back home to Durban later that afternoon with a storm cloud hanging over me. The whole way back I didn't turn the radio on; I sat there fuming at myself! *Why didn't I have a business card? Who doesn't carry his stupid business card? Was I so unprofessional that I didn't carry my business card?* Of all the people in the world who would venture to ask me for a business card, it happened to have been Nelson Mandela!

A short time later, I was back at the Mandela Foundation for another shoot. I came armed with a whole bunch of business cards. Mandela was meeting with a well-known president that morning, and twice I had tried to slip my card to Mandela with no luck. I didn't try again after that. Even today, when I am extremely nervous talking with a group of business people, I like to tease them and ask if Madiba had ever asked any of them for their business card.

Most days, Mandela was in a relaxed mood. He generally loved to talk and was always looking around to see what was going on. He had a plush lounge and a fireplace adjacent to his office desk at the Mandela Foundation. Many times, I'd find myself standing or kneeling in the opposite corner, waiting for things to happen.

The usual game plan when Mandela was meeting with guests was for Zelda to give me the sign to come in to the office. I would greet Mandela and move off to my spot about 10 feet from where Mandela was seated and wait. A short while later Zelda would return with the guest and the day would begin.

One morning, I walked into his office, went over to Madiba, shook his hand and asked how he was. Madiba was in fine spirits, and replied,

"I'm very good, very good."

I loved how, when in a good mood, he would sniff and eagerly look around at what was going on. I'm often asked what I miss most about him. For me, it was those small mannerisms that he had, like the sniffing or the way he greeted people. I enjoyed how he would hang his one hand over the arm of the chair and roll his wrist, whilst moving his fingers.

Once or twice, when I got up close, I noticed that he had missed a few spots whilst shaving that morning and there'd be a tuft of white facial hair on his chin, totally white, just poking out. I didn't get a close up shot that day, but it reminded me that he was just an old man who, like us, had good days and bad days.

Madiba never took aging too seriously. When it came to his old age, he was always ready with a joke that made fun of his great age. On one occasion, I was kneeling right next to him. I'm not sure what I was doing, but Zelda came up to him and gently brushed away some hairs that had fallen on his shoulder. I remember Madiba looking at me and saying,

"You know, they just keep falling out." Everyone laughed.

Madiba beamed a brilliant smile and looked straight into the camera. I took a fantastic shot. What a beautiful morning.

On the days that I photographed Madiba, I would make sure to get the focus correct through the viewfinder. Using the available light was very unforgiving when it came to pin-sharp images, so I did my best to at least get the focus right. Most times, I wasn't really listening to what Madiba and his guest were talking about. I was making sure to focus my lens on Madiba's eyes, not his nose or ears. Nothing was more irritating for me than to get a beautiful portrait, only to later discover that I had accidentally focused on his nose.

Sometimes, we had to choreograph the morning's photo shoot. As far as possible, we wouldn't instruct Mandela directly. The last thing we wanted was to direct his personal time with friends or guests. Usually, I'd have a quick discussion with Zelda about the shoot and we'd get on with it.

I laughed one morning; I was explaining the photo shoot to Zelda, whilst demonstrating my ideas. I indicated that I would 'shoot' Mandela from a particular angle. A bodyguard, who was standing not more than five feet away, heard the word 'shoot' and bounded over, all concerned. We all laughed, but that guard watched me like a hawk that morning.

Zelda la Grange was an interesting lady. As Mandela's personal assistant, she was the feared and admired gatekeeper. Though I appreciated her work immensely, I didn't ever come to properly understand her. Her sheer commitment and dedication to Nelson Mandela was unwavering, but I never quite knew where I stood with her. I appreciate that I was probably her least favourite person, being a photographer. I was also probably the youngest 'team member' she had to deal with. A few times, I found myself in the firing line and was told to get out, move away, or simply ignored.

It was a game of hit and miss. Away from Mandela, I noticed Zelda tended to keep to herself. She had a few close friends at the Foundation, but in large part, all her energy was focused on taking care of Madiba's best interests. As much as I wanted to punch a brick wall at times, I will be the first to put up my hand and acknowledge that if it were not for her care and commitment, Madiba would have died much sooner.

When Madiba did pass away on the 5th of December 2013, it was a while before I met Zelda again. Perhaps two years had passed, but I still felt that I did not have a sense of closure in our relationship. I certainly did not have anything more than a professional interaction with her, but nevertheless I felt that I perhaps needed to close a chapter properly. The week before Madiba passed away, I had e-mailed her to say that I was thinking of her and though I may not feel the depth of her pain (given her position as his personal assistant and with Madiba being so frail and close to death), I could understand it. It was the only time I had ever been so bold as to share some form of empathy with her. Zelda replied later that same evening, thanking me for my e-mail and acknowledged that it was indeed difficult. She wished me well and that was it. I was grateful for the reply, though.

It wasn't until two years had passed that I got to see her again. By that time, Zelda had written her own book (*Good Morning, Mr Mandela*) about her time working with Mandela as his assistant. She was doing a book tour around the country. I had been invited to a prestigious boy's school in the KwaZulu-Natal Midlands, to address the pupils on my work as a photographer with Nelson Mandela. I arrived on time and was led down to the auditorium where the whole school was already seated, waiting to be addressed.

The Rector of the school was standing outside the building with a small group of people. As I entered the circle, my heart sank and I could feel the rocks sitting heavy in my stomach. Zelda la Grange was there too. No-one had told me she would be there. If I had known, I'd probably have declined visiting that day. I was shocked and immediately defaulted to my old self, as if I was back at the Mandela Foundation. We shook hands, and we actually hugged. Zelda was all smiles and said it was good to see me again. I wasn't too sure about that.

Fortunately, the Rector ushered us into the auditorium, so there wasn't time to dwell on what I had walked into. Zelda was to speak first, as she had a pressing engagement to attend a little later. I, in the meantime, slipped into the darkened auditorium and seated myself with the head prefects in the back row.

I was pleasantly surprised by the talk Zelda gave. The boys loved it and enjoyed asking various questions of her about Mandela. Seeing that I was tucked away and probably out of clear sight from the stage, I put up my hand to ask a question too. Zelda indicated I could speak and from out of the darkness I asked if it was true that she had kept Her Majesty the Queen of England on hold on the telephone. Zelda laughed and politely said,

"Well the rule is, if you call Mandela, you're expected to wait."

As Zelda was about to move on to the next question, she suddenly stopped and asked for the house lights to be turned back on. The auditorium lights went on and Zelda moved from the podium to the very front edge of the stage. She looked out at the audience and questioned the boys about who had asked that last question.

I began to panic. The boys turned to look at me. Zelda cupped her hands over her eyes to block out the stage lights and took a long, hard look.

"Oh, I see," she said, before turning to step back behind to podium. Everyone was dead quite. Something was up. Zelda looked out over everyone and then continued:

"Boys, I want you all to turn around and to take a good look at that person in the back row, who asked that last question."

I wanted to curl up and die. *What was she doing? Why was she about to ridicule me or treat me like she did all those years ago, especially in front of all these boys? I'd never forgive her.* In fact, I was ready for a fight.

The whole school and all the teachers were now looking directly at me.

"You see, gentlemen," Zelda continued, "that person is pretending he doesn't know anything. I'd like to introduce you all to Matthew Willman. Matthew and I worked together for many years at the Nelson Mandela Foundation. We know each other, and he also knew Mandela too. His photographs of Nelson Mandela are some of the best that have ever been taken of Madiba, and Madiba liked him."

The audience erupted into applause like I'd never heard before. Boys whistled, some stood. All I could do was to sit looking through the clapping sea of hands, at Zelda on the stage, with the biggest smile of relief. In front of the whole school, Zelda had truly honoured me, she had truly affirmed me. There was no-one else, not even Mandela's wife or the President of South Africa, who could have said those words to release me from all those years of pent up anguish and insecurity. It was beautiful and the boys kept on clapping.

The Rector adjourned for 15 minutes, allowing time for Zelda to leave. I made my way to the front to say goodbye to her. I gave her a hug and thanked her for her kind words. I didn't want to show her how much they meant, but it had really changed everything for me. As we were talking, Zelda asked me if we had ever had a photo taken together. I thought for a moment and said,

"No." So she handed her camera to the Rector and together, with mended bridges and eager school boys gathered around, we took a few photos to remember the day.

Who knows what made Zelda do what she did that morning? But I hope if she ever reads this chapter, that she truly knows that she made a difference in my life, which I will forever cherish.

....

CHAPTER 7

TRIPPING OVER PRESIDENTS!

If only life gave us reruns. I'd watch my failures over and over to reaffirm that my commitment to life and discovery was authentic, fallible and real.

The first president I ever encountered was former US President Jimmy Carter. That didn't go too badly. I was out in a township, photographing a new low cost housing development being built by the international organisation, Habitat for Humanity. President Carter was inside inspecting one of the units, and outside quite a formidable press detail had gathered. I had heard that the former president would be helping out with his wife, the former first lady, Roselyn Carter. As usual, I was excited to see what all the fuss was about. This was my first interaction with secret service agents – fortunately, it didn't end too badly. Whilst President Carter was working inside one of the houses, his security detail kept watch as a large gathering of press photographers and media jostled for a prime spot to get their shot when President Carter walked out the front door.

I don't know what it was, but one of the security guards had it in for me. Each time I reached the front, he'd say I was too close. I'd shy away and allow the more skilled journalists to muscle their way past me, sucking me towards the back. I was a complete novice at this, as I was so used to obeying instructions that I did what I was told, even if I didn't need to. That's why I was at the back of the mob and not up front jostling for the best spot. Call it what you like, but I became angry. The mob was so dense I couldn't squeeze back in-between the tightly packed shoulders. I dropped to my hands and knees and crawled to the front. I withstood the odd kick here and there from whoever was up above, but I made it to the front in the nick of time. I looked up, only to have that same agent peering down at me. But my timing was spot on. The president walked out and from between the agent's legs I snapped a wonderful shot looking up from ground-level, as President Carter smiled at the crowds. The only person in the image looking down at me was his lovely wife, Roselyn. She too had a smile on her face, but hers was perhaps a little confused at what she was looking at between the legs of her security detail! As soon as the president had moved off, the same secret service agent I had beaten to get to the front looked down at me and, pointing his finger helplessly, told me not to do that again!

President Kenneth Kaunda of Zambia is a man well-respected and loved, not only by his own people in Zambia, but across Africa. He is hailed as one of the great fathers of independence, having been the first black African president of the newly independent nation of Zambia in 1964. I love Zambia. There is truly a hardworking self-respect embodied in all the Zambians I have met. The country has competitions for the cleanest town or city, which in my books is Livingstone, by a long shot. My point is there's national pride and people want to work; they want to educate themselves. I love the place.

Unfortunately for me, President Kaunda was no hero of mine whilst I was growing up. I had been taught to fear this 'terror from the north,' a black man whose government assisted the terrorist ANC (African National Congress). I remember my aunt narrating how during the 1950s, Kenneth Kaunda hid in her house whilst running from the police and eventually jumped out the back window to escape arrest. All this changed when I attended a conference in 2001. I was alone and as the proceedings got underway, a group of four people came in and sat in front of me. The room was dark, so I couldn't quite make out who they were. After about an hour, the lights came back on and we adjourned for a bit. It was then, to my complete shock, that I saw who was sitting in front of me. I immediately hated the man, this terrorist! But then I thought, *Hold on, he's not rushing away; he's just sitting there.* I leant forward politely and introduced myself.

"Mr President, may I have a word with you?" The two guards on either side of him sat upright, ready for anything. President Kaunda peered around, his eyes fixed on me.

"Yes, come, my son." He indicated to the guard to make room for me. So I stood up and went to sit next to him.

"Mr President, my whole life I have been brought up to believe you are an evil man."

President Kaunda laughed:

"And who told you that?"

"My family and those who left Zambia when you came to power."

Kaunda just nodded, so I carried on:

"President Kaunda, if I ever get the chance to talk to others about you, what can I tell them, so that I know everything I've been taught was wrong?"

"Yes, my son; you see, this world is full of misconceptions."

I didn't take my eyes off him. I was transfixed.

"My whole life," Kaunda continued, "even way back when I was a little boy, my parents taught me to have faith and believe in a God who protects us from the wild animals of Africa, a Christian God. My people also travelled through the vast areas of what was then Tanganyika and Nyasaland to find a home in what is today Zambia."

"So your message is?" I interrupted.

"Love ... You must tell those who hate to find love and, most importantly, to forgive. I have spent my life trying to forgive and to love and so must you."

We shook hands, smiled at each other and I walked away.

Something broke inside me that day. I couldn't quite put my finger on it, but I was learning to discover my own path, my own experiences about this continent and its peoples.

I have already told you about meeting President Thabo Mbeki at the funeral of former President PW Botha and how Mbeki thought I was Botha's grandson, so I won't go back there. Mbeki's successor, Jacob Zuma, is an entirely different individual, if ever there was one. For approximately five years, I had done numerous shoots with President Zuma. The access I had and the interaction, although formal, was close. Yet I was always saddened by the fact that this man never once greeted me or offered to shake my hand. This made me angry. I have washed my hands of any further work with him and removed myself from ever photographing this man again. History will judge his legacy, and that will depend on who succeeds him in South Africa.

In Paris, as an invited guest of Monsieur Hubert Hermès, I attend a gala dinner with the then president of France, Nicolas Sarkozy, and his beautiful wife, Carla Bruni. In Johannesburg, there was former US President Bill Clinton, in Cape Town President FW de Klerk, and in Canberra, whilst exhibiting my work on HIV and AIDS in the Australian Parliament, the then Prime Minister, Mr John Howard, walked past my exhibition. I called out to him in the hopes he would come over to see my exhibition, but I was shocked at how his security detail completely swamped him and a member of his staff reprimanded the prime minister, saying that he would be breaking parliamentary protocol if he allowed me to come over to him, as I was a complete stranger. I've honestly never seen a president man-handled and literally pushed to move on by a member of his own security detail. The last I saw of Prime Minister Howard was him looking back to me, waving apologetically. So, who knows what that was all about?

A little later that day, the Governor-General of the Commonwealth of Australia, Mr Michael Jeffery, refused to see my exhibit on HIV and AIDS in South Africa until my own president (at that time President Thabo Mbeki) admitted that HIV caused AIDS. This infuriated me, because that was exactly the reason why I was there and why more attention needed to be given to this issue. I spent a week in the firing line of everyone who dared step into my space. All except a man named Bob Brown, the then leader of the Greens Party. He stopped by for five minutes. He had to leave in order to vote for some act they were opposing; he handed me a signed copy of his book and never returned. Perhaps one of the craziest weeks of my life!

I have also kept a president waiting for half an hour. One morning, my photo shoot with Nelson Mandela ran over the intended time. When I left the office, a very formal gentleman in a suit was standing waiting. He must have been standing there for quite a while. I hardly greeted him; I could sense this next meeting had nothing to do with me, so I hurried out the main door. The man I had kept waiting was the then exiled president of Haiti, Jean-Bertrand Aristide.

There is one interaction that will live with me for the rest of my life. When I think back on it now, I burst out laughing and then feel a twinge of guilt and utter disbelief at my absolute stupidity.

In 2014, I had been invited to attend and speak at a very high profile event in Dublin, Ireland. Other guest speakers included the Irish Prime Minister, Mary Robinson, UN Secretary General Kofi Annan, together with an array of presidents from South America, philanthropists and entertainers. It was, for me, an absolutely surreal experience. I had been invited to speak at a few plenary sessions that had been organised to run alongside these towering figures in the social and political spheres of our global community.

The conference opened with quite some fanfare. As a guest speaker, I was asked to join the other speakers on stage as a sort of celebrity showcase of the who's who at the conference. The event organisers wanted to introduce each of us individually, to add excitement and keep the audience in suspense to know who would appear next.

There were about thirty of us waiting in the wings, grouped together, each group having six guest speakers. The backstage production crew told us they were running ten minutes late, so we all just had to stand by. In front of me, Bob Geldof chatted away to Boris Becker. They were quite into it, so I didn't bother interrupting. I turned around to see a tall, well-dressed man behind me. I stuck out my hand and introduced myself as Matthew Willman from South Africa, there to give the talk that evening on Nelson Mandela.

This man shook my hand firmly and without telling me his

name, proceeded to comment on South Africa.

"You're from South Africa?"

"Yes, sir, born and bred."

"Tell me now, I hear you have a few problems in South Africa?"

I was a bit taken aback by such a question. Whenever I'm off the continent, I immediately become 'Africa Proud'. So, in hindsight, my reaction to this man got things off on the wrong note.

In reply, I asked what country he was from.

"My apologies; I'm from Mexico."

Before he could continue, I set off on a tirade about the problems Mexico was facing. Perhaps I should have stopped there, but I didn't. I said that I believed that Mexico would never win its battle with the drug trade and that the government was in on the whole thing! I may even have suggested that it was my belief that their president was receiving backhanders from these cartels in order to traffic the drugs and money in and out of Mexico. I had gone too far.

The man from Mexico folded his hands, obviously taking very seriously what I had just said.

"Leadership is a difficult task to be given. Perhaps someday I will look back and see where things could have been done better in my country."

I was confused. *Who was this man and why was he speaking like that? Why was he wearing a small Mexican flag on the lapel of his suit?* When I looked around I noticed what looked like Mexican bodyguards.

"Excuse me sir, who did you say you were?"

With that, a large hand reached out to me and whilst shaking it, he introduced himself.

"My name is Vicente Fox, former President of Mexico."

I was devastated. I had not only embarrassed myself, but I had brought shame on South Africa, and Nelson Mandela, whom I was there to represent! We all talk about speaking truth to power, and whilst watching TV we throw out bold assertions that if we were ever to meet such high profile people, we would speak our minds. Well I did just that, and it's not pretty. Few words can describe my complete shock and how utterly devastated I was for what I had just said about the drug problem in his country.

I apologised profusely. I literally held my head in my hands in shame and embarrassment. I was completely out of my depth and had tripped up just when I thought I had become used to being around such influential people.

President Fox laughed. He put his hand on my shoulder and said he would love to invite me to Mexico one day as his guest! To which I replied that I would never visit Mexico, as I was sure that after this insult I would be sent home in a body bag. He wasn't too sure how to react to that answer.

Before I lost complete control, I was quite literally saved by the bell. One of the assistant producers backstage interrupted us, and just like that we were all hurried out onto the stage to face the multitude of cheering crowds, mass media, loud music, TV cameras, flash-lights and the press. All I could think of was that there wasn't a chance I was ever going to visit Mexico after my huge *faux pas*! Just like all the other celebrities, I stood, grinning a useless smile, and waved as if I was enjoying the moment. *What on earth was I even doing here?!*

....

CHAPTER 8

NOTHING TO LOSE

At every point, I had to keep reminding myself why I was doing what I was doing. I knew I was in trouble if that focus was lost.

Have you ever considered how hard it was to try to get to meet Nelson Mandela? Take a moment, and in your own thoughts ask yourself what you would have done or how you would have gone about it. Imagine yourself sitting in your lounge, by the pool or out shopping for groceries, and you suddenly get this idea that you really want to meet Nelson Mandela and you are going to do all you can to make that happen! Then what? That's the part I want to know. What's the first thought that comes to mind. How you would imagine yourself carrying out that plan?

I know of people who have met Mandela without much effort. They are the lucky souls who, whilst going about their lives, bumped into him in a hotel in America or on the street in

England. Even in South Africa, there are wonderful stories of these astonishing chance encounters that people relate over and over around dinner tables, sports fields and on social media.

I'm convinced that the story of Nelson Mandela no longer lies with those in power or influence. The true legacy and history of Nelson Mandela is now firmly held by the common man. Ordinary citizens will perpetuate these seemingly small encounters, which when told and networked over time, will form a composite picture of what his life really meant to people. I've never met anyone who had a bad experience with Mandela. Perhaps there are? Each story I've heard is told with a sense of excitement, joy, laughter and meaning. Books have been written purely on people's personal encounters with him. Even this book is one big series of encounters.

It seemed to me that the obvious place to start, when attempting to meet Mandela, was by writing letters. Over the months and years, they became many, many letters. I wrote that I was a young South African inspired by Mandela, and if there was any opportunity to meet him, I would travel to Johannesburg at his convenience. In fact, I used that phrase many times. Every second month or so, I would receive a reply. The Nelson Mandela Foundation would thank me for my letter, they would say how appreciative Mr Mandela was to have received my letter, but unfortunately his schedule was full. The last part varied a bit over the years. Replies included being busy, resting, being abroad or writing his sequel to *Long Walk to Freedom*. One of the last letters I received from them stated that Mandela no longer lived in Johannesburg. They were not making excuses. Mandela had indeed moved down to Qunu, the rural village where he grew up. I was loath to go down there, some 430km from my home. It wasn't so much the drive as it was the impenetrable design of his house and security features. You literally turn off the main freeway and not more than 10 meters away, on the side of the road, are enormous gates with a police check-point. There was nowhere to park, as it is illegal to stop and make camp at the side of a national road. I know this because I had tried a few times.

The house in Qunu was designed to shield much of it from the main road and it is positioned to look out onto the rolling hills. Mandela could sit and watch the constantly changing weather or his Nguni cattle being looked after by herd boys. I was to discover that the entrance was via a winding road. It didn't lead directly to the house, but wound its way to the main parking area along-side the residential complex. If anyone stood at the front gate and peered through, all you would see were a few thick bushes down a road that made tight corners left and right. So, basically, you saw nothing.

It wasn't until I was commissioned to work with Mandela's eldest grandson, Mandla Mandela, on his installation as Chief of Mvezo, that those huge, wrought iron gates at Qunu finally rolled open and I had the opportunity to go in. However, that was a number of years after I first engaged with Mandela.

The complex is actually two separate houses. Initially, Mandela had asked for an exact replica of the house he lived in for 14 months at Victor Verster Prison. To most people this sounds crazy: why would anyone want a replica of your prison to become the design of your new home? The truth is Mandela liked the layout; it was a simple house, not too big to move around in. Remember, it was the first normal place he had lived in for over 25 years. The only thing that was not added to the home in Qunu was the swimming pool. Mandela never liked swimming anyway. I knew that because of my friendship with Mr Jack Swart, the last of three prison wardens who looked after Mandela whilst he was in prison for 27 years. Jack was also Mandela's personal chef at the Victor

Verster Prison house and looked after any of his needs until his eventual release.

I have spent a few nights at the house in Qunu. It's mid-boggling how they have managed to build an exact copy. I've also spent a lot of time at the prison house outside of Paarl in the Western Cape, and when waking up in the Qunu house, it feels like I am 1 000km further south, in the countryside outside Cape Town. It's a very strange feeling indeed.

What I liked about the house in Qunu is that it was a real, working household. When I have stayed there, it was always a hive of activity, people cooking, family coming and going, and I was never without someone to talk to. Yet the prison house at Victor Verster is devoid of life; it is empty and very lonely. It's a space where time stands still. All the windows are shut, the curtains are drawn and it still echoes a sad and painful past. The prison house was left as it was the day Mandela walked to freedom on the 11th of February 1990. The trees are now very tall, and without proper care the bushes are now growing high above the walls. The lemon bushes near the back gate are all large trees and the fig tree Mandela planted is having a second go at life. The initial trunk grew old, withered and died, but now there are new branches coming up. I don't like the house, but I do love its role at a pivotal time in South Africa's history.

I have digressed a bit.

For about eight years, I wrote to the Nelson Mandela Foundation. I could not tell you whether I wrote thirty or fifty letters. I certainly received many letters in reply: so many that I could have wallpapered my bedroom with them. My point is I was simply another unknown, troublesome individual, who thought that by being polite I could meet this great man. The replies from the Mandela Foundation were always polite and very gracious. I was even told that Mandela extended his best wishes to me and hoped I was well. Somehow, I don't think, of the thousands and thousands of letters he received, that he ever saw mine.

Whilst writing letters, I hatched another plan. Maybe if I went out to meet people who knew him, then maybe I could ask them to take me to him. Sadly, no-one was prepared to offer any help. The list was long and the replies I did receive basically said they never used their position to provide access to Mandela. I understood. But I have to laugh that of all those I had asked, it was one of Mandela's sworn enemies, former apartheid President PW Botha who, although he couldn't make the contact, gave me the telephone number of Madiba's wife, Graça Machel, in Maputo, Mozambique. So I called. Someone answered the phone, speaking Portuguese. I asked to speak to Graça Machel, and explained that I was calling from Durban, South Africa. The lady, who spoke in broken English, asked if I knew Mrs Machel personally. Of course, I could not pretend to know her so I said no, and just like that she hung up. I didn't call back. I had never before felt so intrusive of someone's private life. I scratched 'contacting via friends' off my list of approaches.

It is important to add that all of this was happening over a period of months and even years. I would be lying if I said I was always having a good time. There were days of utter despair. You pin your hopes on one opportunity, imagining success. You write a letter that sounds perfect and then nothing, not even a reply. There were days I'd drag myself off to my job waiting tables, feeling numb. I'd have breaks with the others on the back step at the kitchen door and just sit there listening to the pathetic stories of their lives. They had no dreams, nothing to lift their conversation. They were saving for nothing. This said, I have such great respect for anyone who lives and works at that level in society and has a dream or an ambition to improve their lot, not by loud, boastful ideas and dreams, but by silent progression of saving, making plans and focusing on the unseen, wishing for the day of emancipation.

David Beckham had a role to play too. I learnt that the English football team were coming to South Africa to play against South Africa's Bafana Bafana football team at King's Park Stadium in Durban. I knew the stadium well. I had been through all the back rooms and corridors where the players change rooms are. I also knew side entrances that eventually lead to the main tunnel, which leads out on to the field. I had photographed at the stadium many times. All this gave me an idea. *Maybe I could ask David Beckham to take me to see Mandela?*

I managed to get a press pass to photograph a training session of the South African team. I waited patiently for that to end as I had been told that the English team would be arriving immediately afterwards. Right on time, the tour bus pulled up and famous names passed within a few metres of me: Michael Owen, Rio Ferdinand, Sole Campbell, Phil Neville and of course, leading the team, David Beckham. I watched them playing for ten minutes before some very British sounding staff told us we had to leave as this was a private practice session and no media was allowed. I was broken. Making my way with the others through the tunnel, I hung back. In a split second, I ducked into the change-room toilet. I turned off the lights and shut the door.

A long time passed. I opened the main door ever so slightly, just enough to see what was happening outside. It was painfully dark and boring. Peering through the crack in the door, I could see members of the team leaving the field, heading back to the bus. In panic, I hauled myself out of the toilet cubical and literally threw myself into the middle of the English football team. I didn't have a clue who I was looking at. I was gunning for one man: David Beckham.

I caught up with him as he trailed behind the others, signing autographs for kids who had been allowed to watch. I was a bit late. He had already started to walk briskly back to the bus. With no decorum or dignity, I reached him, shook his hand and desperately asked if there was any possibility I could go with him to meet Mandela. I had heard that the following day the whole team were being given an audience with Mandela, in Johannesburg. Beckham looked at me in disbelief. He stopped walking, signed a few more signatures, looked up at me again as I had not moved, and said,

"Sorry, mate, but I can't help."

I decided that night I had to give up. I just had to let it all go. Yes, it had been an adventure. Yes, I'd met some truly wonderful people along the way, but the truth was I was running out of steam. I had no money to keep pretending I could go to meet Mandela. I didn't even own a car. My 250cc Suzuki bike was leaking oil and I had nothing in the bank. I had come to the end of my drive. I knew I was at the end because, whilst watching David Beckham walking away, shaking hands with a swarm of media tracking him, I had to ask a friend for a lift back home.

I felt I hadn't failed only myself, I had failed my family. My siblings were all well on their way with careers in law, medicine and science, and where was I? I was twenty two years old and was feeling that I still had nothing to show for it; all I had was a three-year diploma in photography. I thought that maybe I just needed to press 'reset', forget about Mandela, take responsibility for my life, toughen up, and start taking on work as a photographer of weddings and family portraits. I told myself that if I was good, maybe I'd get lucky and shoot some sports event or get to fly to

Cape Town to shoot Table Mountain. I didn't care, I was tired, I had lost touch with reality; I needed to change something!

I went back to normal, daily life. I drank with friends, spent weekends getting on with life, trying to make things work. It was a relief to be released from things that had limited me from living in the present, not always running around spending money on things that didn't work. At socials events, I found myself amusing others with stories of the people I had met. I made friends easily; I always had a story to share and people loved it. I'd have a good time and then the next morning I'd get up and carry on as if the previous night hadn't happened. I didn't want to think about any of it. I was all the way down in Durban, Mandela was up in Johannesburg, and absolutely nothing I had done in the past seven years had gotten me any closer to meeting him.

One morning, after a particularly heavy night of socialising, dancing and mayhem, I woke up smelling of the night before. I fumbled about in my bedroom and headed to the shower. It was raining outside and after a few minutes of standing under the jet of water, the whole bathroom was a sauna. I had a lot on my mind. *What was I missing? Surely there was something I had not done that would at least get the attention of the Mandela Foundation.* I hated that I still kept thinking about this whole mess I was in. I was all lathered up with soap, I turned to face the shower nozzle and it hit me. *Photographs! The answer had been staring me in the face the whole time: it was right in my hands.* I had studied photography, but it had never dawned on me that photography would be the catalyst.

I must have panicked, because I leapt out the shower, grabbed a towel and whilst drying myself, I smelled my towel. It was full of soap. In all the excitement of these new thoughts, I had forgotten to rinse off the soap.

It felt like I was holding a cheque for a million dollars, and if I let it go, I would lose it forever. I needed to stay with this thought. *How could photography help to make this Mandela issue any better?*

I went online and began to search in Google for all the places I knew of that pertained to Mandela's life. There were places I had never even heard about, names I couldn't pronounce. I began to read about them, what they were about and why they played significant roles in Mandela's life.

I sat gazing out of the window for ages, trying to piece together how I could use my photography to get me to Mandela. Other photographers before me had extensively covered the locations pertinent to Mandela's life. *But I had not photographed those places, so there was still a chance. Maybe if I went out and began to document some of these places I had a chance. If I sent images instead of letters to the Mandela Foundation, there was a chance they might take notice.*

One place stood out above all the others: Robben Island.

I don't know what ideas you thought of when I asked the question about reaching Mandela at the beginning of this chapter. I bet none of you thought about starting with what you already have in your hands. I should have started from my strength; I should have started with photography.

CHAPTER 9

ROBBEN ISLAND

A place that time and humanity lost track of.

I didn't know where to look. I lay flat on my back, my hands gripping the metal legs of a row of benches that were bolted to the floor. All I could do was to lie there looking up at the sky, peering through the wooden slats. Far above me, totally oblivious to what was happening on this tiny little boat, a seagull winged its way out across the bay. Effortless, perfectly suited to its environment out there where the vast oceans rise and fall and where only the bravest dare.

I was a complete wreck. I lost sight of my bird and returned to reality. Our boat lurched, crashing head first into wave after thumping wave. As it moved forward, it flopped sideways and then rolled back, pulling itself upright, only to rise up and crash forward again as it spluttered its way across the bay from Cape Town to a distant point I thought would never come.

Through the salty spray of Atlantic sea water, which engulfed everything, I could smell that ghastly diesel smoke belching out the exhausts from the engine room below. I cursed myself for ever having stepped on this boat. If my will power had been strong enough, I'd have hauled myself overboard. Dying was better than the helplessness I felt being crucified by the sea, vomiting across the top deck and losing all dignity. That day, I swore that I'd never, ever visit Robben Island again. Never!

The boat eventually rounded the island and slipped into the mouth of the harbour; it had beaten the sea and now chugged effortlessly into Murray's Bay Harbour as it had done for over 50 years. From my horizontal position, still anchored beneath the benches, I could make out the harbour walls and, in the distance, one of the guard towers of Robben Island Maximum Security Prison.

I have lost track of how many times I have been to the island. Each time I go, I promise myself never to visit again. I hate that 40-minute boat ride. It is always rough, due to the fact that the boat has to cut across a current that swirls around between the island and the mainland.

After everyone, including the captain of the boat had disembarked, I crawled up onto the jetty, rolled onto the concrete landing and lay there. Bolted to the harbour walls were large, black and white archival photographs of former prisoners lined up in chains, about to begin their life sentences on this forgotten piece of land out in the windswept Atlantic sea, 8 miles off the coast of Southern Africa. I looked at the strength of those men lined up, none of them rolling on the floor, gasping for life, trying to recover from seasickness.

The rest of the team were all waiting for me, ready to start our work, which would keep us busy for the next few days on the island. I hobbled over to the group and there, standing without a care in the world, breathing in the smells of the harbour, was Ahmed Kathrada. He nodded a polite hello to me, looked around and said we should go.

Ahmed Kathrada, or 'Kathy' as he was fondly known, spent 18 years on Robben Island. He too had been imprisoned there for life with Nelson Mandela, after the infamous Rivonia Trial in 1964. We had met many times over the years, but I had not yet had the privilege of retracing the intimate details of his life as a political prisoner on the island. The memory of special occasions like this particular shoot, evoke a number of life-changing experiences that the island gave me over the years.

As much as I hate the island, there are days that I find myself reflecting on a deep sense of peace out there, exploring its forgotten reaches. I was privileged enough to document the island over a period of 18 months early on in my career, for the Nelson Mandela Foundation and the Robben Island Museum. When nothing was happening, I'd take my camera, a bottle of water and go for long walks out along the far reaches of the island, far away from the prison and the tourists. When I felt I was far enough away, I'd clamber along the jagged rocks, find a spot and spend the afternoon flicking shells and pebbles into tidal pools, or just sit alone, gazing out onto the vast South Atlantic, peering deep into its endless memory.

I remember one day I returned to the island with PW Botha, South Africa's former apartheid president. We came to the island on the original *Dias* boat, the same boat that for years had ferried political prisoners to and from the mainland.

Together, PW and I walked along the jetty of Murray's Bay Harbour. No-one noticed us; maybe they didn't even care? We walked under the archway welcoming visitors to Robben Island

and headed straight up to the main entrance of the prison. When nobody was around, we walked along the cold stone corridors, turning left and stepping out into the B Section courtyard. A short walk up a ramp leads you into the holding cells where Nelson Mandela and the other Rivonia trialists spent 18 years, hidden away from the world. In the adjoining cell block, former prisoners were waiting for me to photograph them, but first I had some unfinished business with PW Botha.

From my pocket, I took the key that had locked away men like Mandela, Kathrada and Sisulu. I opened the door to Mandela's cell and walked inside with former President PW Botha.

The former president had died the previous year, and I had returned to the island for the sole purpose of bringing a story full circle. Inside an old shopping bag, I carried a hat that had belonged to the former president. When PW Botha died in 2006, his widow had given me this piece of memorabilia. I had a story to tell and it involved Nelson Mandela's prison cell and PW Botha's hat.

In 1982, PW Botha, then president, had offered to release Nelson Mandela, on condition Mandela gave up armed resistance. Of course, Mandela refused. During those tumultuous years of PW Botha's leadership, there had been an increase of secret meetings between the National Party and the African National Congress. On those occasions, Mandela had to remove his prison clothes, change into a suit and then leave his prison cell in order to leave the island for private meetings with the government and even with PW Botha himself.

PW Botha had never visited Robben Island, nor ever came to see Mandela in prison. During the years that I got to know PW Botha, I had often asked him if I could take him to Robben Island, to show him around. The answer was always the same:

"Why would I want to go there?"

With no-one else around, I took the old hat and placed it on the shelf in the cell. I stepped back and welcomed PW Botha to Mandela's office on Robben Island. In doing so, I was completing a journey that had begun when Mandela was still on the island in the 1980s. With PW Botha's hat, inside Mandela's prison cell, I welcomed this former apartheid president to his very first meeting with Nelson Mandela on Robben Island. The image I took on that day is hauntingly beautiful.

Of all the stories from my time on the island, one stands out most because it nearly cost me my life.

I had been photographing near the only piece of land on the island not owned by the government. The Church of the Good Shepherd was owned and maintained by the Anglican Church, and, like most things on the island, it too was looking tired and weathered, having been beaten by South Atlantic storms for decades.

Around noon the sun was high in the sky, so I decided to head back to the prison to see what was happening there. As you approach the prison, a large guard tower anchors the scene. I noticed the door to the tower was open. I didn't think anything of it, but went right in and proceeded to clamber up the stairs to the top. The view was fantastic: I could see the whole island and peer right into the prison complex with all its sections, courtyards, holding cells and corridors. Right below me was the C section courtyard. I watched as a rather large group of tourists came out into the yard. I'd done that tour many times, just to listen to the stories and to remind myself of the realities of prison life. At first, I didn't take much notice of the crowd below, but when I really looked properly, I noticed everyone was gathered around two men. Using my camera lens as binoculars I could see that the one man was Ahmed Kathrada and the other was a well-dressed man wearing an Indian turban. Someone must have noticed me perched up in the tower with the long photo lens. I must have looked like a sniper. Pandemonium broke out. People were shouting and the crowd made a quick escape back into the cells.

I panicked, swung away from the window ledge and threw myself back down the staircase, bashing my camera on the railings. I was in trouble now; they had seen me and were probably expecting the worst. I reached the ground floor landing as the guards entered. I screamed out that I was a photographer and that I was unarmed. I stood there in utter shock. Immediately, I was pulled alongside the wall, my camera taken away and I was patted down. By then, there was a group of South African and Indian police agents swarming around. What a mess. I didn't even have my identity card on me. All I had was my camera. My bag was in the admin block on the other side of the prison.

I was told to sit on the floor whilst they went to find someone who could identify me. A prison official came round the corner to assist in the situation that had developed. Fortunately, I knew the man. I didn't say anything. We looked at each other and he immediately got on his cell phone to call someone. He chatted for a bit and then handed the phone to me.

"It's your boss."

Palesa Morudu had given me the credentials to have access to photograph independently on the island. She had been sitting in her office in Cape Town when her phone rang with the news that the Indian security police had almost shot me on sight. I don't know what was worse: sitting under heavy guard with guns trained on me, surrounded by irate security police or to having this woman read me the riot act and tell me how I could have been killed with no questions asked.

What had actually happened was that I had walked into the

middle of an official state visit by the Prime Minister of India, Mr Manmohan Singh. Ahmed Kathrada was escorting him and his delegation around that day, and I happened to be in the wrong place at the wrong time. I was held by the police until the delegation had left the island, then without much fuss, I was told I could go.

Of the many names around the world I have been privileged to have worked with, it is perhaps those men who were sentenced to long-term imprisonment that I have come to admire and respect the most. I have journeyed long and hard to not only photograph the people and places that collectively make up large parts of South Africa's history, but I have also made sure to bring myself as close as possible to what their experiences must have felt like. My work has brought me alongside rural communities, people living in humble dwellings, experiencing how something as simple as drinking a cup of clean water, requires long walks to communal water pumps. Cooking food requires daily treks into the forest to harvest wood. In urban areas, the camera has afforded me an opportunity to document individuals living in townships, catching public transport, walking long distances to work 10 hour days, arriving home late in the evening after walking back from the taxi ranks or bus stops that return them to the townships. I am under no illusion that life is simple and easy for the people of Africa. Yet, of all these, it has been my personal experience of working with long-serving political prisoners on Robben Island, that I value most.

When I first visited Robben Island, I was more interested in capturing iconic images of the island. I wasn't particularly interested in the individual stories of other prisoners outside of Mandela's 18 years on the island. I guess I was so focused on Mandela, that at first I excluded a large part of what the island itself had symbolised over the centuries. Over the years, as I matured, I found myself returning to the island to work with individuals, to watch how they responded to the prison walls they knew and remembered so well. I count myself privileged to have been afforded time alone on Robben Island with Ahmed Kathrada and Aubrey Mokoape. It was a privilege to spend a few days with Denis Goldberg, who, being white, was separated from his fellow Rivonia trialists to serve out his prison term in Pretoria Maximum Security Prison.

Incarceration does things to you; it changes you. For some, it refines you, whilst for others, it destroys you. I have watched how these men behave, the little things that show how their minds adapted to the cold, iron bars and concrete walls of prison. It's been fascinating to witness how each one had to deal with isolation and loneliness; how they had to wrestle with their convictions. I have watched how, although scared and wounded, the triumph of the human spirit has overcome the injustice of imprisonment. Mandela recognised this. It is why, upon returning to the island, he placed a rock in the middle of the lime quarry as a symbol of his forgiveness. He recognised that even though he was a free man, he would remain imprisoned by his captors if he did not choose to forgive. These are not men who go about with their hearts on their sleeves, for all to see. You have to spend time with them before you begin to recognise their pain.

In 2007, I returned to Robben Island with the former leader of the Black Consciousness Movement and Chairman of the Pan Africanist Congress, Dr Aubrey Mokoape. During my time with him on the island, we walked side by side with his wife, Gwen, through the corridors and holding cells where he and fellow prisoners were held. Dr Mokoape took us through to the isolation cells. Once inside, you are suddenly overwhelmed by the terrifying darkness; a single window, five meters above, lets in the faintest light. Mrs Mokaope refused to enter. Concerned that she was upset, I left Dr Mokoape inside and went to find Gwen. We chatted for a bit, but then she stopped me.

"Listen, can you hear that?" Gwen had her hand on my shoulder.

We both stopped to listen.

Inside the isolation cell, we heard laughter.

"Is that Dr Mokoape?"

Gwen was silent at first, but then looking at me, she replied, "Yes, it's his only way of releasing the pain and anguish."

Few words can adequately describe witnessing the expression of torment and pain. Sometimes, you just have to allow space and time.

Ahmed Kathrada only ever showed me his vulnerable side once, when we were with a few small children. Nothing was more important to him than to interact lovingly with children. I was fortunate to be commissioned to photograph Mr Kathrada for the book *A Simple Freedom*. I was out in the lime quarry, alone with Mr Kathrada or 'Kathy' as we used to call him. I did my best not to set up any of the photos. I merely followed, watched and waited for the right moment to capture images that were authentic. I learnt that when you have spent so much time on your own, you become drawn to that isolation. Sitting on a rock at the entrance to the lime quarry, I watched as 'Kathy' moved away and went off, walking in the quarry alone.

This is how things were for me. There have been astounding moments, photographing intimate details of this forgotten place that for over 400 years had been a site of isolation, hatred and death; and there were moments in between when I was faced with things that challenged me to answer my own issues and questions.

Whenever I step off the concrete jetty onto the boat to take me back to the mainland, I hesitate for a moment, because I never know if this will be my last time on the island.

I remember reading how, a few years before his death, Mandela used to say how he missed the solitude and privacy the island had afforded him. I didn't quite understand at the time I read that, but now I do.

....

CHAPTER 10

A ROAD LESS TRAVELLED

*I used to think that I needed to tell everyone what I was
doing. But now I know some things are best kept a secret.*

Somewhere in the middle of rural North America, there is
a road that I spent years trying to find. The road had no
historic significance, it does not connect to a large, important city, nor can it take you anywhere important. In fact, this
road merely passes through farmlands, planted on each side with
cornfields.

In 1994, the road earned a place in Hollywood history for its
ten-second appearance in the film *Shawshank Redemption*.

There is a scene in Frank Darabont's interpretation of Stephen
King's novella, *Rita Hayworth and the Shawshank Redemption*,
where we witness the character, 'Red', played by Morgan Freeman.
After forty years in prison, Red is trying to accept his own institu-
tionalisation. There are many times Freeman's character considers

suicide, but remembering his friend's words to him many years previously, Red begins to believe in hope, and sets out to try find his friend in Zihuatanejo, Mexico. Before he heads to Mexico, he needs to find something his friend had secretly buried for him alongside a rock wall, next to an old oak tree in a hayfield.

For the first time in this classic story of love, hope and getting even, with a sliver of hope and trust in his friend, Red sets out to buy a compass. We witness the transformation of a soul finding new life, heading out into the unknown.

The scene opens with Morgan Freeman coming up over a ridge on the back of an old, red pickup truck. At the junction, the truck slows to a stop and Freeman gets out. He thanks the driver and the truck continues on its journey. In the next few seconds of the film, we witness someone who is afraid, alone and with only a few words lingering in his head, starting out on this road to find his friend.

For years, I scoured websites that provided tours to the various set locations in the film without luck. None of them could tell me where in the world this tiny scene had been shot. I kept a notepad on my desk and began to list the locations where the film was made. I read somewhere that many of the rural farm scenes were filmed near the small town of Butler, Ohio. Using Google Earth, I pinpointed this tiny speck of a town, literally in the middle of Ohio, south of Mansfield. Once I'd found it, I noted its position and then the real fun started. There are four roads leading in and out of Butler. I knew one of those roads would eventually lead me to the farm road I was looking for. As the weeks turned into months, I would return to Butler on Google Earth, pick a road and then meticulously move the map fifty meters at a time, looking at the street view. It was painfully slow going and many times I gave up and didn't return to Butler for weeks or months.

It wasn't until mid-June in 2013, that I picked up the chase again. I had printed a photograph of the film scene and kept flicking back and forth to reconcile what I was looking at on Google Earth with the landscape in the photo. Late one night, I decided to spend a few minutes examining street views where the four roads split. My landmark was an old wooden church. When I zoomed in and out, I noticed that there was a tiny road running east-west, linking the two arterial roads into Butler a few miles north of the town. In my head, I could see the junction where Morgan Freeman climbed down from the red pickup truck. As I trawled along, following the road from an elevation of some one hundred metres, a similar junction flashed up on the computer screen. This was interesting. I zoomed out and noticed two farm-houses; their positions matched the scene in the photo. I immedi-ately opened 'Street View'. I felt a sense of wonder and delight, as if something as revered as the Sistine Chapel was being revealed to me for the first time, on a brilliantly sunny, cloudless day. Through the portal of Google Earth, I was looking down the road I had so long hoped to find. I looked at the co-ordinates and smiled, knowing I had found the location. The name was clear for all to see: Snyder Road.

I printed out the Google Earth map, highlighted the roads off Interstate 71 to Snyder road, and pinned it on my wall. Now all I needed was to save some money and wait for the opportunity to pack my bags and go.

Months crawled by. I would walk past the map to Butler, Ohio, trying to figure out how on earth I was going to get there. Some days, I'd stop and stare at the map, imagining who lived there, what the weather was like, did the scenery look exactly like it was in the film? It held my imagination and kept me fired up, deter-mined to go there one day.

Little did I know that not far from Butler, Ohio, in the city of Cincinnati, some three hours' drive south-west, a group of people had been trying for months to make contact with Nelson Mandela's family. The National Underground Railroad Freedom Center had announced that they were awarding Mr Mandela their highest award for Freedom, the 'Conductor Award'. Although this award would be made posthumously, the honour and respect afforded to Mr Mandela, even in his passing, signified the depth of admiration for Nelson Mandela around the world.

Sitting in Cologne, Germany, I was oblivious that any of this was going on. I was in the middle of an exhibition. The past few days had been cold, and I was eager to head home and get back into life in sunny South Africa.

On my way back to the hotel, a few blocks from the gallery, my phone rang. It was an old childhood friend, who was now living in Geneva, Switzerland. Lindsay and I shared many things most people would find boring, but most of all we loved to laugh and make fun of life's little foibles. It was good to chat and catch up, but there was a sense of urgency in her voice. I had reached the hotel; not much was happening in the lobby, so I found a sofa in the corner and sat down to carry on the conversation.

"Matthew, I need you to call someone in America. His name is John Pepper, and I told him you would be able to help in getting him in contact with Mandela's family."

I wasn't too sure what it was all about, but trusting Lindsay, I said I would call. I was always hesitant about my ability to make contacts, especially when it came to influential people. I took down Mr Pepper's number, said goodbye and sat in the chair, looking out at the pelting rain that was making my day even worse. I had nothing to do. I checked my watch; realising that the USA should be up and about by now, I dialled the number and waited.

A secretary answered the phone. I explained who I was. I think she was a little confused, as I mentioned I was South African but that I was calling from Germany. It all came out wrong in the end. Fortunately, she told me to hold and she put me through to Mr Pepper.

Mr Pepper and I greeted each other. His voice sounded firm but relaxed; he thanked me for calling him and said how wonderful it was that I knew Lindsay. He proceeded to tell me how the National Underground Railroad Freedom Center, of which he was chairman, were battling to contact the Mandela family to invite them to receive the award on Mandela's behalf. I agreed that finding channels to anyone within the Mandela family was difficult, but that they should actually go through his foundation in Johannesburg. I said I could certainly put him in contact with their CEO. We chatted for a few more minutes, exchanged e-mail addresses and hung up.

Over the next few weeks, upon my return to South Africa, I made the introductions and became quite actively involved in arrangements for the ceremony that was planned to happen in September of the same year. I shared my story and involvement with Mr Pepper, and it became obvious that images of Madiba would certainly be a wonderful additional tribute in sharing who Nelson Mandela was with the people of Cincinnati.

So it happened that I travelled to Cincinnati later that year with fifteen of my photographic prints to share in the events.

So much was going on with work and imminent trips to Ethiopia and Kenya that I didn't immediately have time to allow the excitement to build. Neither had something else dawned on me yet. About a week into confirming the trip and my involvement, I walked into my spare room to get a few things. I closed the cupboard door and the page I had stuck to it fell off and lodged itself between the bed and the bed stand. Irritated, I fished around on the floor, thinking it was an old reminder about something or other. I picked it up, stood up and peered at the page. There, circled in yellow highlighter pen, was the town of Butler. I glanced at the bottom of the map and saw that the City of Cincinnati is situated right on the Ohio River. I measured a gap of about 2 inches on the map between Cincinnati and Butler and calculated that it would probably be a three hour drive.

I figured out that I would have an opening of two days to get a car and drive from Cincinnati to Butler on the Interstate 71. *Could this be the opportunity I had been waiting for?* Indeed it was. That single page quickly became the focus of an entire wall covered in screen grabs from the film, various route maps, distances and GPS settings.

I'm always amazed how often sound is the missing puzzle piece we forget about in any experience. A friend, Laura, travelled with me, and we left early, heading north-east on Interstate 71, knowing that within 50 miles I would see familiar landmarks I had recorded on Google Earth pointing the way to Snyder Road. Once I turned off Interstate 71, I felt as if I had been there before. I knew every turn and building along the road. Before we rounded a corner, I knew what we would see. Magically, familiar sights appeared: the old wooden church, a monument, a low-slung farm gate, a beautifully kept farmhouse. It was like a gift waiting to be unwrapped. You only get one first impression. After 9 000 miles, three flights and a three hour car trip we crested the top of the hill. I was waiting for that red pick-up truck to come trundling past. We pulled off the road and I walked into my own imagination. Laura sat quietly in the car, allowing me some time alone. I stood in the middle of the road and re-enacted the scene in my mind's eye. I watched as Morgan Freeman climbed off the red truck and waved goodbye. I even stepped back, moving out of Morgan Freeman's way and turned to watch him make his way down that road to find that tree.

In my dreams, I had imagined doing all of this, but what brought the reality of it home and gave this experience true fulfilment was the sound around me. It was exactly as I remembered it in the film: the heat, the sunlight and most of all, the distant noise of late summer cicada beetles ringing out across the corn fields.

I suspect many of you want to know if I found the oak tree described by Andy Dufresne (Tim Robbins) in the movie. It felt as if that road wouldn't be complete without touching that tree.

Without telling Laura, I pointed the car in the direction we needed to follow. We wound our way through the fields, making a few left turns, and pulled up alongside a field on the right-hand side of the road. The sun was out and there she was, the oak tree, as tall and impressive as the day she was filmed. There was a long fence, littered with signs threatening all sorts of prosecution to keep visitors away from this famous location.

I remembered that over the hill and out of sight of the road was a creek. With my camera around my neck and my mind filled with expectation, I walked along the fence line to the boundary of the farm, and then proceeded down the hill towards the creek. I crossed the stagnant water and following the water's edge, I made my way back towards the tree.

In my hand I held an image of the scene where the camera moves in behind Morgan Freeman, then tilts up, revealing the old rock wall and the oak tree in the middle of a hayfield. I made my way along the river, walked across a few fallen branches. Hauling myself up, holding the trunk of a large tree, I peered through the bushes as the scene unfolded before me. It was astonishing. There was absolutely no-one around, the main road was somewhere on the other side of the tree, allowing me complete privacy and time alone to absorb all the sounds that surrounded me.

Imagination is a powerful tool. Apart from Laura still waiting patiently in the car, there was not a soul in the world who knew where I was. My home and family were some 9 000 miles away, on the east coast of Southern Africa; they would be going about their daily lives, perhaps making dinner. In the townships, coal fires were clogging the evening air whilst families huddled together for warmth. Lions were stirring out on the open plains, preparing the pride for the hunt that night. Yet here I sat under an old oak tree, my back against an old rock wall, born and bred in the heart and soul of Africa, living out an almighty dream. None of this would have meant anything if it were not for the determination and power of imagination.

I sat quietly, my head resting against the old oak. I knew that the second I stood up and made my way back to the car; all this would exist only as a memory. I knew there would be things I wouldn't remember. With my camera on the ground next to me, I just sat. I watched as the breeze-blown gnats danced and jumped above the wild grasses. I listened as the cicada beetles whined along the edges of the forest. I smiled to myself, looking at the remains of that old rock wall, picturing Morgan Freeman kneeling on the ground somewhere very near to where I was sitting, as he looked for that hidden treasure his friend had promised to him all those years earlier. The sun sparkled through the thick tangle of oak leaves; it was blissfully peaceful.

Usually, I find a leaf or a stone to take home as a keepsake, but this time I didn't. I wanted only the memory of me sitting under that tree, resting, without a care in the world.

....

CHAPTER 11

LISTEN AND LEARN

No better way to learn than to discover new horizons on your own.

I t's easy to remember how awesome it was to work with Nelson Mandela. I got to be in his presence, listen to him speak, watch his mannerisms, enjoy how he laughed and joked, offered advice or a story or two for his visitor. Simply amazing.

Yet working around this legendary man was demanding. I always likened it to being in a hurricane. When I was alone with him, it was peaceful, but I rarely had moments when I felt completely confident or relaxed. As a photographer working in such a closed space, I quickly realised that I was stepping into an abnormal world, with stringent rules and protocols. Of course, Mandela himself was perhaps oblivious to it all; or rather, he had become used to all the attention he garnered. In the very early years, when I was 24 or 25, I was constantly making mistakes.

Simple things like standing in the wrong place, coming in too close, or hanging around when I wasn't supposed to. It was a trial by fire. There was no-one to hold my hand and guide me through it all. I made it up as I went along. Most of my learning during those days was through observing and listening to how things worked.

Firstly, there was the machine around Madiba, those that were immediately responsible to Mandela. This included his personal assistant, Zelda la Grange, Mandela's third wife, Graça Machel, Mandela's personal bodyguards, house manager, cook and various assistants. There was always a process or a decorum which I recognised quickly. I was never in the company of these people in a casual sense. Whenever I was there, I had a specific job to focus on. There was never an occasion when I was simply hanging around, waiting for something to happen. I think only family members were allowed the privilege to sit back, talk and enjoy whatever happened next.

Outside of the inner circle there was a second challenge: the media – those journalists, photographers and videographers who had their own agenda. The Mandela Foundation had an excellent relationship with many in the press corps and they all knew that if anyone fell foul of the rules, they'd be out.

So, in front of me I was dealing with the inner circle and behind me was this intimidating media machine that did not take lightly to some unknown photographer walking in with Mandela or going through to his office ahead of the rest of them. I certainly wasn't their friend. In the early days, I once made matters worse by agreeing to do an interview with a national newspaper. I expressly told the journalist that any reference to me alongside Mandela was as a commissioned photographer to the Nelson Mandela Foundation. You can imagine my horror come Saturday, waking to a front page entitled: 'Mandela's personal photographer speaks out.' There are a few moments in my life where dying would have been easier than what I was about to face at the Mandela Foundation. It was a disaster. I was isolated and pushed to the side and didn't get to photograph for the Mandela Foundation for many months. They were gentle with me but very firm. I had allowed my five minutes of fame to destroy (not completely) my reputation with the Foundation. It took a long time to repair. Even now, when I am interviewed I'm very cautious and guarded. Often, when a journalist comes across me they are amazed to learn that I even exist, because they have never even heard of me. I smile, because then I know that we did our job well. We went about our work staying away from the media and any claim to fame. In the media there is no protection on any public platform. Your own words can be twisted and used against you, even words you've never said.

I was not brought up in the world of competitive journalism. I have always somehow managed to get my images and stories into the media somewhere and find a direct connection with the subject at hand.

Initially, I thought the media could be trusted, but as time went on I began to realise something else was at play. Working for the Nelson Mandela Foundation, I was able to witness from the side-lines how the media behaved. Many times, the focus of their pack-like behaviour was Zelda la Grange.

I don't think you'd believe how challenging her role as Nelson Mandela's personal assistant was, unless you saw for yourself the nonsense Zelda had to put up with, almost on a daily basis. It was unrelenting. I didn't dare approach Zelda on my own, as I always thought that she saw the presence of any photographer as a potential threat to the smooth running of Madiba's schedule, so I respectfully kept my distance. Zelda was the guardian and everyone else, no matter who they were, had to go through her to gain access to Nelson Mandela. A number of people have already written about contributing factors and tried to analyse how and why Zelda la Grange came to be so influential in her role alongside Nelson Mandela. The only comment I will make in this regard is that when Nelson Mandela retired from office as State President of South Africa, the entire weight of his fame and legacy was handed over to Zelda and Professor Jakes Gerwel. With no prior experience, she never once backed away, but took each and every challenge personally and created a secure and protective environment for Mandela. Zelda helped to create a platform upon which he was able to have a voice and to go about his commitment to humanity long into his retirement. By no means was Zelda always right, but I will be the first to stand up and defend her.

When I look back at this well-oiled, professional team around Nelson Mandela I realise that the man we all came to know and love was in part due to the protection and care that people like Zelda la Grange gave him. Mandela was afforded the space and attention to march on, trusting that these people had his back.

Every now and then Madiba would drop a bombshell that left people scratching their heads. Whilst walking through an exhibition, Madiba stopped at a photograph recorded on the day of his inauguration on the 10th of May 1994. The image showed Mandela standing to attention and behind him were a few high ranking military personnel. Whilst the group gathered around Madiba were patting themselves on the back, enjoying their exhibition, Mandela looked closely at the photo and then turned to the group and asked who those generals in the photo were.

You could hear a pin drop. No-one in the group could tell Madiba the names of the generals. One by one, they added their two cents worth, looking at each other red-faced, trying to answer the question. Whilst all that was going on, Madiba turned towards me; whether he was looking for someone more important to talk to than me, I have no idea. I had been standing close to Madiba getting images, so as he turned around, I happened to be closest. He looked at me and said under his breath,

"You know, they almost got us. They almost got us." As quickly as he had uttered those words, he proceeded to move on to the next image.

Each time I'm called to forgive or endure some hardship, I'm reminded of his words that morning. Madiba never once forgot the magnitude of opposition he had been up against, especially with the police and military might of the National Party government.

At other times, a few quiet words here and there from Madiba gave me certainty that, even in his advanced age, he was inquisitive and his mind was as sharp as a pin.

Late in 2004, the Mandela Foundation was exhibiting a scene of Robben Island in the foyer/exhibition area of the Foundation. Large, wooden boxes that looked like they could have been salvaged from an ancient shipwreck were used as plinths upon which original documents were displayed inside glass cabinets. Madiba was making his way through the installation, stopping here and there before making his way to the auditorium to give a speech. For years, Madiba had walked with the aid of a cane. His personal favourite was a white ivory cane that went everywhere with him.

On passing an exhibit, noticing that the floor was covered in white stones, Madiba stopped, took his white cane and prodded the stones a few times. He pulled himself up straight and looking over to a few of us, he proudly announced that the stones were real. We all laughed, Madiba smiled and muttered,

"I just wanted to know if they were real," and with a big smile on his face he walked into the auditorium to meet the world's press.

If I'm honest, it was tough working around Mandela. I envied those who simply happened upon him and got to hug him or share a story with him. They were oblivious to so much of the tension, the rules and regulations. They had their two minutes of interaction and went on their way to share those moments with the rest of the world.

Quite a few years had passed, and I had completed a significant body of work on Mandela's life that spanned many aspects of his past. I had been called to another private photo shoot in early 2011. It was March, and I had not seen Mandela since October the previous year. It was wonderful to be back and engaged. As usual, I entered the room, I greeted Madiba – a very quick exchange of words – and I stepped back to wait for Zelda to instruct or give permission.

I'm not sure how it came about, but I was in a frustrated mood, wondering how I too could help to make a difference in South Africa. I wasn't too far away from Madiba when I asked him what I could do as a young South African. I knew I was breaking all sorts of rules, but it was an honest question that I had to ask.

Madiba looked out of the window and then, looking back at me, in the most matter of fact way said,

"If you want to remain relevant, you must serve."

It was like a fog had lifted from my mind. *Was it that simple? Is that all I had to do?* Quite obviously, it was.

It wasn't long after that experience that I founded a small charitable foundation to help support young artists, particularly in the fields of photography and dance. With Madiba's words written in my mind, I never looked back. There have been some small but life-changing opportunities when the MW Foundation has given hope to others and allowed young minds to dream.

Maybe all of this, all the stories, adventures and experiences with all their highs and lows, happened so that I could arrive at that one point in my life, in Mandela's office. All I needed was to receive a few words from Nelson Mandela that ultimately opened up a new and focused journey of service. To remain relevant, you must serve.

....

CHAPTER 12

A PLACE IN THE MOUNTAINS

Sometimes the best dreams are those left just as they are, in your imagination.

There's a fascinating world of people and places that exists every moment of every day on this planet. Even now as I sit and type this chapter, I know that there is a large rock lying, as it has done for thousands of years, on the grass-covered, west-facing slopes of the KwaZulu-Natal Drakensburg Mountains. It's there, doing its thing, as it always has done. This rock is perhaps a little more special than, say, the rock a few meters from it, slightly further down the slope. For many years, I knew this rock existed and I made it my goal to find it one day.

In the November of 1994, some seven months after South Africa voted in its first fully democratic elections, which saw Mandela come to power, a script of another sort had been written and was being filmed across South Africa: an adaptation of a book written some fifty years previously.

It was on one of those late summer afternoons, that two actors found themselves sitting together, playing out the final scenes of one of the greatest literary pieces to come out of South Africa. James Earl Jones played the role of Umfundisi (a black African priest), and Sir Richard Harris the role of an English-speaking farmer. The screen adaptation brought to life a story that pre-dated apartheid, written by Alan Paton and entitled, *Cry, the Beloved Country*.

One afternoon, with cameras rolling, an entire film crew found themselves focusing in on the climax of this painful, yet beautiful story: two men sitting on a rock, enacting an almost prophetic story of what would happen to South Africa in years to come.

In December 2011, I had returned from a two-week trip to the Arctic Circle town of Tromsø, in Norway. It had been the dead of winter up there with temperatures hovering around -15°C, and only a few hours of daylight to give an African boy like me the comfort of feeling any sort of normality. The morning after my return, I threw some camping gear into my car and headed for the mountains. I was determined to find that rock. Armed with only a small photo of these two men sitting on the rock and a narrow view of the mountain range behind them to help guide me, I reckoned I had a chance.

The first two days were useless. It was hot, the sun bleached all life and energy out of me, and I only managed a few hours hike each day, which got me nowhere. It wasn't until the third day that I found the energy to push on through the heat. Throughout the afternoon I used the shapes of several mountain ridges to my right as a guide. I knew I was close. I compared the photo in my hands with the vast open reaches of the Central Drakensberg mountain range; things were lining up, but something was still wrong. Why was I not able to line up the folds of the land as they appeared in the photo? It felt like the image had been taken some few hundred meters in mid-air. I looked up, trying to imagine a rock floating with two men sitting on it, suspended some hundred meters above the ridge of the mountain. Whilst looking up, something clicked into place: hold on, I was on the wrong ridge; I needed to be further over. I had my perspective all wrong!

I only had about two hours of good light left. I hurried down the pass, scrambled across a river, and zigzagged my way up a steep, grassy bank. I popped up on top of the ridge, onto a thickly grassed slope bathed in the afternoon sunlight. Dotted around on the hillside were large weathered rocks, scattered about like leftovers from some cataclysmic event in the very distant past. I was close. I made my way a little further to get a better perspective. With photo in hand, I turned around to take a look at the view. Everything finally lined up and there, lying quietly, having remained the same as all those years before, was the rock I had been searching for. It was so beautiful. There it was, hidden away, completely overgrown by thick, wild grass, a rock that millions of eyes had seen, a rock that for years had held my imagination. I knelt down in front of it, filled with such a deep sense of reverence, sheer joy and gratitude for these rare, beautiful moments of finally finding something that, until then, had only existed in my mind. Now, here it was, unleashed from the four walls of the tiny photograph I held in my hand. I was immediately thrown by how small it was in comparison to the majesty and enormous size of the mountains that surrounded this tiny rock. I spent the rest of the afternoon sitting alone on top of the rock, listening to the wind in the grass, watching as tufts of cloud swirled around the peaks of the great 'Barrier of Spears' that we call the Drakensberg mountains.

When I eventually stood up, I moved away from the rock and in my mind I replayed the scene where these two men had come together. I looked back, imagining the whole film crew gathered behind me. But there was only the silence that vast mountains can give. I was alone, and with the sun now set far behind the mountains, I collected my things, placed my hand on the rock one final time, stood up straight and without looking back made my way along the ridge. I followed the path back to where my tent and other campers were getting on with life as if nothing had changed.

Some things in life are perhaps best left to linger within our imagination. Some things don't need to be found. For so long, I had wanted to experience finding that rock, yet when I eventually did find it, I tried to draw out something that simply wasn't there. That rock was not there because of the movie. It was there as nature had intended it to be. It existed as it had always done. When I reached the summit of that hill and found myself gazing upon the scene, I was looking not for reality, but for something that existed only in my own imagination.

....

CHAPTER 13

YET BEING SOMEONE OTHER

The people behind history are people all the same.

There are some truly fascinating people out there. You don't have to do the work I do to appreciate the diversity of human nature, character, personality and outlook in each and every one of us. What makes my work somewhat challenging is that, when someone achieves a measure of fame or notoriety, we immediately build up an idea in our minds of who they are, before we've even met them.

Sometimes introductions go horribly wrong, as it did with the Dalai Lama. It was 2007. The Dalai Lama was in Durban, giving a series of talks. I had been told that I would get the opportunity to meet him as he left the venue. No-one had told me the protocol, so I stood there. After about an hour's wait, the Dalai Lama emerged. His assistant told him to head towards me. We greeted. Smiling, he placed his arms under my elbows to embrace. I had no idea how to embrace conservatively. I panicked. Instead of following his lead, I leant towards him, but unfortunately my position did not allow a smooth embrace. Before I could pull back, I lurched forward and we bashed heads, causing the Dalai Lama to falter. I was stupefied that I had nearly knocked the Dalai Lama unconscious! We held onto each other, he laughed and giggled in his usual manner, whilst I apologised profusely. We chatted for a bit, he laughed often, looking at me over his big glasses. Never once did he let go of my hand.

Brief encounters don't always reveal the true nature and personality of people, but they certainly do go a long way to rewiring perceptions!

Speaking of perceptions, I was absolutely floored, for two reasons, when I had the opportunity to spend the morning with one of the most dynamic, incredibly witty women I am ever likely to meet in my life.

Of all the people in the anti-apartheid movement, Helen Suzman was the true thorn in the side of the National Party. For 33 years, her Progressive Party occupied one seat in parliament. For those 33 years, it was Helen Suzman who was that one, lone voice that spoke out, questioned and completely irritated prime minister after prime minister, president after president, during the years of apartheid. I knew I was in for a treat when I rang the doorbell to her home in Illovo, Johannesburg.

At 86 years of age, she was still going strong. Not more than 10 seconds passed and the door opened. It was wonderful to finally meet one of South Africa's true heroines. Helen Suzman was Mandela's first visitor on Robben Island. Anyone who loves a good story will do well to research what happened on that occasion. But that's a story not for me to tell; you must read it – it's very touching.

It was Helen Suzman who, upon seeing the deplorable conditions of the prisoners on Robben Island, and with the support of the Red Cross, managed to convince the prison authorities to give these men beds. Up until that point, the prisoners had slept on the cold, concrete floor with a couple of stiff blankets and no pillow. It was also Helen Suzman that, on learning Mandela would be visiting his old house in Vilakazi Street in Soweto township after his release, made sure she would go along to greet him as a free man after all those years. The moment was captured forever on film when a photographer snapped the poignant moment when Mandela embraced her. He saw her as a true friend. It is a moment so special it is etched in my mind forever.

So here I was, standing in her doorway, looking down at this same giant of our nation's history. Yet something was not right. In fact, I could see that something was a bit odd. When the door opened and I beamed my big smile, greeting Mrs Suzman, my next reaction was of complete confusion. Initially, I thought I was too early or had the wrong day. Instead of meeting a well-dressed lady, Helen Suzman opened the door still dressed in her nightie. Mrs Suzman smiled and told me to come through. Not wanting to cause further confusion, I stepped inside and had no choice but to follow her down the corridor into a dimly lit room. As I entered the room, Mrs Suzman was already sitting on what looked like a padded table. As I was finally about to say something, Mrs Suzman looked up at me and said,

"You're not my physio, are you?"

I panicked.

"No, Mrs Suzman. It's Matthew Willman. I've come to interview you and take a few portrait images of you this morning."

I have never seen such a calm and orderly manner displayed by someone who had gotten her appointments so horribly wrong.

She tied her gown around her, gave me a brief smile and whilst walking out the room, told me to go into the lounge and she would join me shortly.

Perhaps you can ask me now, what I was thinking? Every preconceived idea I had, was now well and truly snuffed out. *How on earth was I going to explain this one to anyone?*

Helen Suzman re-entered the lounge, this time in more formal attire. She briefly apologised for such a terrible mistake and offered me tea and a tray of blue cupcakes. I certainly didn't want to dwell on the mishap, so I laughed and asked if she was still actively involved with her foundation. It was as if the incident had never happened. We chatted away for a full hour, and it was wonderful. I wanted to experience something of the wit and sharp insight that she was so well-known for. So I went all out and asked her to describe how she fended off all the taunts, snide comments and hate-mail she had received from Nationalist supporters through-out her political years.

"Oh, that's an easy one," she replied. "In fact, I have something I can show you."

She took me into her study off the lounge. She fumbled through a stack of papers piled to one side of her desk.

"Aah, yes, here it is. You may enjoy this one."

Mrs Suzman handed me a letter addressed to her. It was written in Afrikaans on a letterhead of some Afrikaner women's society that obviously supported the National Party without question. It was a polite, but stern letter of disgust at the stance Mrs Suzman was taking in parliament. They felt it was their duty to remind her that it was the Afrikaner nation that had ventured out into the vast, uncharted, wild bushlands of Southern Africa and brought the Bible and Christianity to the savages of Africa.

The letter ended with one question for Mrs Suzman. They

wanted to know what her ancestors had been doing whilst the forefathers of the Afrikaner people were committing their lives to bringing the Word of God to the native people of this country.

I was a bit shocked. *How on earth could anyone reply to a letter like that?*

"Mrs Suzman, how on earth did you reply?"

Helen Suzman laughed and sighed, almost irritated at having received such a letter.

"I replied immediately. I've always wondered what happen to this woman, because I never ever received a letter back from her."

I was now thoroughly intrigued, so I blurted out,

"What on earth did you write back?"

"Oh, that was easy. I thanked the woman for taking the time to write to me. I told her I acknowledged the remarkable history of the Afrikaner people, but then I answered her question with one simple line in reply: 'My ancestors wrote the Bible!' "

I burst out laughing. She was absolutely right, what a wonderful reply. I wanted to hug her for being so sharp and straight to the point. Helen Suzman is Jewish and we all know that Jews wrote the Bible.

This is what I love about my country. Our dynamics, histories, ideologies and stories are all so intricately interwoven that we become this African quilt that makes us so unique, so alive and so beautifully South African.

Don't get me wrong. Apartheid was a horrible blotch on the 20th Century. It should never have happened. Politicians today try their level best to remind us of our divisions and to prop up their leadership by perpetuating racism, hatred and anger to further pull us apart. I reject anything that supports any divisiveness or blanketing of the truth. Apartheid existed so as to undermine the people of South Africa. Anyone who supports the Seven Pillars of

Apartheid needs to re-examine their conscience.

Perhaps one of the most awkward moments I had with Nelson Mandela was a little incident that involved Helen Suzman.

Everyone was gathered in the auditorium of the Nelson Mandela Foundation. I had been sitting on the floor near the main entrance, taking photographs. Madiba was sitting in his usual big, blue wingback chair, facing the gathered audience. I always liked to scan who was in the audience, especially in the front row. So many of our struggle heroes were special guests and given preferential seats, especially if they were personal friends of Madiba. Sitting in the front row, not more than two feet from me, was Helen Suzman. Next to her sat Amina Cachalia, then Graça Machel, Ahmed Kathrada and Denis Goldberg, faces we all knew so well.

Madiba was in high spirits that day. Seated with Madiba was our then president, Thabo Mbeki and former Minister of Finance, Trevor Manuel. As things wrapped up and as protocol dictated, Madiba was always the first to leave the auditorium. It was never a quiet affair; people usually sang or clapped whole-heartedly as Madiba made his way out of the venue. You could see he loved it. As soon as Madiba stood up, I was on my feet. The open space leading to the double doors was not very big, so I knew there would be an opportunity to get some good shots of him as he came past.

With the assistance of President Thabo Mbeki, Madiba began to move towards the door. I noticed he was looking down and not at all the people singing his praises. I took a few images and then, out of respect, I lowered my camera when he came past, so as not to be rude.

Without any forewarning, at the very moment he passed me, Madiba looked up at me, his face broke out into a huge smile and he asked me how I was. I grinned back and said,

"I'm so well, Madiba," and Madiba moved on out the door.

With Madiba gone and people still singing and clapping, I relaxed to take in the morning's event. Helen Suzman, who had been standing right next to me, looked up at me and in her very matter of fact way, promptly asked,

"What makes you so special?"

I burst out laughing. I had no idea. Helen Suzman smiled, and I asked her if she had a lift back home after the event. She said she would be okay; she was staying for a cup of tea and then Mamphela Ramphele was taking her home.

This was the extraordinary world, or bubble, I walked in and out of whilst working for the Mandela Foundation. Working in close proximity to Mandela, I came to know a wide array of impressive people whose lives had, in their own right, helped to move this country forward.

Of course, many international personalities came to visit at the Mandela Foundation offices. My work was not limited only to the commission I was given by the Foundation. I went out in my own capacity to engage and photograph many of these same individuals for my own portfolio. I would often set up shoots at their homes or their own foundations. These occasions were always memorable, so when they did come by the Mandela Foundation, we already knew one another. Many of them called me by nicknames that somehow stuck. If Madiba called me 'Prince Harry', Ahmed Kathrada referred to me as his 'cheeky boy'. Rivonia trialist, Denis Goldberg used to call me 'Matt,' whilst Inkatha Freedom Party leader, Chief Mangosuthu Buthelezi, kept calling me 'Thomas More'. He was not going mad; he simply knew that I had attended a small private school called Thomas More College in KwaZulu-Natal with his grandson, so I guess the association stuck.

At the time, it was all part and parcel of my work – I didn't see it as anything abnormal. I was living my dream, feeling for the first time that I was actually a part of what was happening in South Africa. To those who know me well, I've always expressed the feeling that, because I grew up in a predominantly white suburb outside of Durban, I was somewhat removed from the change that occurred in the country. I always desired to get out there and to feel a part of my country. So my work on Robben Island, in the Inanda Valley, Eastern Cape or Johannesburg gave me the satisfaction that I was seeing it all for myself. I was meeting and interacting with many of the key role-players of the last 60 years of South Africa's history.

The biggest problem or challenge was that all these people were well into their eighties. Madiba was in his 90s, and those who had been with him since the 1940s were also around that age or fast approaching it. Every year that went by saw more and more of these interesting people passing away. Sometimes, their deaths would come only a few months after I had photographed them with Madiba at the Foundation. We had our work cut out for us. We were racing against the clock, and literally every month narrowed the chance of working with and documenting these living legends.

When I returned home, it was not to a world of fame, high society or people with whom I could share what I was doing. No-one really cared. I returned home to a town where people were so focused on just getting by, holding down a job, looking after their kids, trying to make their own lives work. My neighbours and family had no concept of this fascinating world or that the people they had learnt about in school or seen on television were people I was engaging with almost weekly, across this country.

....

CHAPTER 14

MAKING CHOICES

At some point, we all make a choice that changes the course of our entire lives.

I must have been about 13 years old when I experienced my first awakening to the very serious political situation in South Africa. It was 1992. I was enjoying life in my little bubble, when one school day I sensed that things were not as they should be. I remember a buzz of hushed conversations between the teachers. They would smile at us but then return to their private conversations. They were distracted. I was sure something was happening, something much bigger than my little world. My classroom was on the third floor and had a nice view looking out onto a sports field. On clear mornings, we could see a sliver of the Indian Ocean and, if we were really lucky, a container ship anchored offshore.

Our teacher was also in an unusual mood that day. I remember looking up from my class work to see her standing looking out the window, lost in another world. Her arms were folded and there was a tense, almost pensive expression on her face. I looked over the heads of the other pupils, trying to see what she was looking at. A tractor was mowing the grass on the sports field, but her gaze was focused somewhere out beyond the school, maybe even beyond the ocean on the horizon. Something must have disturbed her thoughts; she very quickly returned to what was happening in the classroom.

Other kids must have noticed what was going on, and kids being kids, asked her if she was okay. She smiled, which was reassuring, but she also mumbled something that left a knot in my stomach. She said that South Africa was at a very important crossroads and some very important people were making decisions about our future.

For the past two years, my tiny little world had been slowly merging with the reality of what was happening in South Africa. I took it for granted that when we went into town to do our daily grocery shopping or to enjoy a coffee, our bags had to be put through a metal detector or inspected by some security guard at every shop entrance. It had become so common that I thought it was normal practice.

Soon after our tea break, we were led into the library and made to sit in rows in front of the television set, to watch an announcement by the state president of South Africa, Mr FW de Klerk.

I immediately recognised who he was. For some reason, he had become intertwined with the memory of my family Christmas holiday of 1989/90 in Cape Town. Less than a week after we returned home, I knew something big had happened. This man, who was now talking on the television, looking at us, was the same man everyone had made a fuss about because of a speech he'd made at the opening of parliament on the 2nd of February 1990, when he had announced the decision to release Nelson Mandela from prison and that the ban on the ANC and other organisations was rescinded.

Now, two years later, sitting there in front of the television, looking up at him, it was as if he was right there in the library. President de Klerk was announcing that white South Africans had unanimously voted 'YES' to end the apartheid system of government which had been in place since 1948. From his tone, I sensed that whatever this apartheid system of government was, it was no longer going to be the way the country would be run. *Surely this was a good thing, so why was everyone at school acting so nervously?*

Not long after my awakening, the reality of it all came knocking.

It was the school holidays and I had taken my bicycle into town to post a few letters. The streets were busy, people getting on with things as usual. I parked my bike and chained it to the back of a telephone booth outside the post office and went inside. Not more than ten minutes had passed when, without warning, an almighty explosion rocked the whole building. The sound wave thumped against my chest, causing instant confusion. It felt as if someone was attacking me from all sides. People panicked. The doors to the post office burst open and people scrambled to get out, completely blocking the main road outside.

It was surreal. I dashed out the post office and followed curious onlookers around the corner to the local magistrate courts. A plume of dust and smoke floated up through two enormous ficus trees. Bricks and rubble were scattered down the steps and across the road. The blast had jettisoned pieces of the court entrance all over. I later discovered that a limpet mine had been planted in one of the rubbish bins near the entrance to the courts. I had no idea if anyone had been killed or injured, but I do remember cycling home in great excitement. It was as if I had discovered a

121

new energy. All this talk on television was real; I had seen it for myself. My community and world was now a dangerous place. As a young boy, that prospect thrilled me more with excitement than fear.

Apart from my complete naivety about the seriousness of it all, the only changes I noticed in the months that followed was that every single rubbish bin in and around town had been removed.

I tell you that story as a platform to describe the context in which my work with President FW de Klerk took place.

I have had the privilege of working with de Klerk many times during the course of my ambitious journey into the heart of South Africa. I remember skulking around him at former State President PW Botha's funeral, hoping like hell he wouldn't recognise me. Fortunately, that was in the early days, and given the multitude of people he engages with on a daily basis, I'm hopeful he didn't recognise me.

My first interaction with FW de Klerk was an interview I had secured as part of a Master's Degree programme I had been actively engaged with. I was granted 30 minutes with de Klerk at his foundation offices in Panorama, outside of Cape Town. Like my initial interview with Archbishop Desmond Tutu, I still had a long way to go in understanding protocols and engaging professionally. The main thing I gained from this time with de Klerk was the opportunity to take some powerful portraits, one of which became the front cover of de Klerk's biography. But it wasn't until many years later that I truly came to appreciate who this man was.

I was commissioned by the FW de Klerk Foundation to spend some time with de Klerk, capturing a series of images that built on his legacy. I was given *carte blanche* on how I wanted to approach this commission visually. For weeks, I worked on ideas, angles, lighting and type of portraits. I was weary of trying to record timeless pieces of an eighty-year-old man that would immediately become dated. So I had to keep thinking.

A few years before, I had been commissioned to photograph a series of archived documents over at the National Department of Archives and Heraldry in Pretoria, which is located behind the Union Buildings. Whilst spending endless hours, working under pressure to get through boxes and boxes of documents pertaining to Mandela's history, I came across a file that read 'President de Klerk, Opening of Parliament, 2 February 1990'.

I opened it and inside the folder found approximately six neatly typed pages. I sat back and, still wearing the compulsory gloves, took some time to read the document. Nothing really struck me at first, but on about page three, one particular paragraph leapt off the page and smacked me in the face.

This was the original document that President de Klerk took to the podium in parliament. From these pages he had read the speech that would forever change the course of South Africa.

Half way down the page, in paragraph three, were the two sentences that blew apart apartheid forever. They read:

'I wish to put it plainly that the government has taken a firm decision to release Mr Mandela unconditionally. I am serious about bringing this matter to finality without delay.'

I sat on that stool for ages, holding those documents. De Klerk himself had read from these same pages. So I made sure to photograph each page and to include it in the archives I was building for the Mandela Foundation.

About a week before I was to start my work with de Klerk, I suddenly remembered that experience in Pretoria and knew I had an opportunity to create something very special.

After chatting with de Klerk about my idea, he asked me how I'd like him to sit for his photos. I smiled and said however he liked, because I wasn't going to do any formal portraits that morning. Both de Klerk and Brenda, his assistant, looked at me in surprise. Without saying a word, I moved his chair to the corner of his desk, politely cleared a few things and asked him to sit. Once he was seated, I handed him some paper and asked him if he would write for me. Of course, this was all a little bemusing and came as a surprise to him. He asked me what I wanted him to write and I said,

"Your speech, sir; the one from 1990, during the opening of parliament."

De Klerk was shocked. He asked if I meant the whole speech; I laughed and apologised, and explained,

"No, sir, only two sentences from that speech you made on the 2nd of February 1990."

I thought at first he wasn't going to do it, because he immediately stood up again. *Maybe I had gone too far?* I quickly apologised, thinking I had said something wrong. But everything was well; he said that if I wanted to record something like that, it was best that it was written using one of his special fountain pens.

Back in his chair, de Klerk became serious. He wanted to see the two sentences, photocopies of which I had brought along. He marked out the spacing on the blank page, looked many times at the typed words and then began to write. While he wrote, I moved in closer and began to take photographs. The lighting was perfect. It was unbelievable; I watched as each word was imprinted onto the page, how the black ink contrasted with the white paper, reliving that historic occasion. As de Klerk wrote, I could hear his voice in every word. I was recreating history. As he signed and dated the two sentences '2nd of February 1990' this man's bravery in dismantling this grand apartheid system once and for all, was a revelation. And there he was, sitting right next to me.

I took many more photographs that morning, including a whole series of portraits, but nothing came close to the image of de Klerk physically writing those words in his own hand.

As I mentioned earlier, President de Klerk's offices are situated in Panorama, outside of Cape Town. From his desk, you look out across the whole of the Cape Flats, with Table Mountain and the city bowl isolated in the corner of the southern tip of Africa. I had expended so much energy that morning, I was tired. Somehow President de Klerk and I ended up both standing, staring out the window. We didn't say anything, but we shared a moment of significance, two souls standing there, looking out the window.

Before I became too familiar, I turned away to begin packing my things. Without a word, de Klerk turned around to head into another room. I gathered my belongings and headed out to the reception, as I needed to chat with Brenda about the shoot. Brenda emerged from his office and said,

"Mr de Klerk would like to say goodbye."

A little surprised, I went back into his office. We shook hands, had a quick photo taken of us together to mark the occasion, and I headed for the door. I was a bit unsettled; I felt in my heart that I needed to say something. So I turned around and looking at President de Klerk, I stood up tall and said,

"Mr President, thank you for what you have done for South Africa."

It was so spontaneous and unplanned that had I had time to think about what I wanted to do, I probably wouldn't have said anything. But I did, and it came from a place deep inside, a kind of upwelling that needed to be expressed, an affirmation of what I had learnt over so many years that had now been spoken. He nodded and smiled, and without any expectation I turned and left the room. That was the last time I saw him.

....

CHAPTER 15

WHEN THE WORLD APPLAUDS

When the world applauds, listen to the spirit within that got you there in the first place.

I do not take failure well. In fact, you don't want to be anywhere near me when things go wrong. I wallow in the recesses of my mind, allowing depression to swamp my thoughts. This is because I treat every endeavour as one that could make or break in my career.

I create mental images of my work long before I actually go out to photograph them. These become so real in my mind that the eventual act of photographing is simply the completion of the process. In addition, I realise that certain opportunities present themselves only once, and have to be grasped instantly to be achieved.

As I write this, I am smiling to myself because I'm aware that during the years I spent trying to meet Mandela, all I ever experienced was failure. In the days when I was receiving rejection letters from the Nelson Mandela Foundation, I was so convinced that each new letter I received from them was another definite no, that I wouldn't open it for ages. I was constantly trying to ignore what reality was screaming at me. I handled failure so much better back then. I had nothing to lose, so whenever any good news or any advancement came it was a bonus. As my portfolio of images developed, the body of work became something to be reckoned with. A much bigger picture of our history emerged and I realised that there were gaps in the story that I still needed to fill in visually.

I have collated an exhibition that has travelled the world with me. It's a magnificent collection of photographic prints drawn from my time documenting the story of Nelson Mandela's life. It affords audiences an intimate and thought-provoking insight into this man's life. I know that I would never have created this exhibition if I hadn't captured one particular image.

During the years that I photographed Mandela and ventured into the many places that pertained to his life, there was one very specific image that I desperately wanted to capture. For six years, I had suggested to the Nelson Mandela Foundation the idea of photographing such an image. I was desperate for their permission to shoot it. Over the years, I had taken many images detailing Madiba's hands, including the now iconic open palm photograph. But it was a portrait study of Mandela's 'Amandla' fist that I really desired to photograph. I felt that being granted permission to take this one image would validate my worth and authority in the competitive world of photography and particularly as a photographer of Nelson Mandela. I would lie awake at night thinking about it. That one image would complete the body of work that I had laboured over for all those years. At the back of my mind, I was aware that time was running out. Madiba wasn't getting any younger and I didn't know when or even if I would ever have another opportunity to photograph him.

The Foundation never gave an outright 'No' when I asked, but equally and painfully, there was never a definitive 'Yes'. I found myself frustrated and increasingly moody as I tried to let go of the whole idea.

One of the other shoots I felt was important to do, was of the original rondavel (African hut) where Mandela was reputed to have been born. It is located in the rural village of Mvezo. I needed that image and I knew that with the looming installation of the new Chief of Mvezo, Mr Mandla Mandela, that door would be closed forever. I had what I felt was a good working relationship with Mandla. At times, that relationship was strained as I became caught between two sides.

Early on in my endeavours to capture images of Mvezo, I had driven five hours down to the Eastern Cape and spent the night in a less than adequate roadside hotel, in order to be ready and waiting bright and early the next morning for my shoot at Mvezo. Just after 11pm the night before the shoot, Mandla Mandela called and said that he was refusing me permission to come to Mvezo, and that was that. Instead of getting the shot I really wanted, I ended up driving home in a foul mood. It took me weeks to get over that. As with many other missed opportunities, I chose to wait. Eventually, access came with the kind permission of Nelson Mandela himself. I was afforded the opportunity to create a hauntingly beautiful landscape photograph of the footprint of Madiba's birthplace. Today, as I prophetically surmised, the original landscape beyond the rondavel has been redeveloped. I am glad that the earlier tranquillity and atmosphere of that precious piece of history has been recorded forever.

It wasn't only my pursuit of Mandela that repeatedly challenged and transformed me. For years, I asked Madiba's wife, Graça Machel for the pleasure of doing a portrait shoot with her, but the opportunity never materialised. I had photographed Graça Machel many times over the years, but I was not afforded the privilege of a private photoshoot. Similarly, I missed the opportunity to shoot portraits of Fidel Castro and Muammar Gaddafi. I had all the correct contacts, but in the end, I simply entered the game too late. Castro became ill and closed himself off from the world, and Gaddafi died in a trench alongside a road in Libya, shortly after I had been in touch with his brother.

Sometimes, after a lot of work and achievement, you look up and the whole world is applauding. I've mentioned before that the years from 2003 to 2010 were a wonderful time at the Mandela Foundation. The whole world came knocking on Mandela's door, wanting to be seen and heard in the company of this world-renowned man. When a president's popular support was waning, he'd make a bee-line for Mandela, hoping to increase his support back home. I'm sure Mandela was aware of this and I'm sure they were surprised by his matter of fact questions when they walked into his office. I wasn't privy to what went on behind closed doors, but watching various personalities come and go I could imagine what occurred.

One of the most anticipated events during this period was the 466/64 Concert on World AIDS Day, 2007. I was fortunate to be a part of it. The day before the concert took place on the 1st of December, an amazing group of local and international musicians, singers and songwriters gathered at the Mandela Foundation. They were there to meet with Madiba, to go through the next day's events, relax and feel welcomed. We gathered in the auditorium. I positioned myself off to one side, facing the audience, photographing and observing. It was wonderful to see the faces of artists whose music I'd listened to my whole life. I definitely felt the least of all those gathered there that morning.

2007 was the first year that the Mandela Foundation would be integrating the new 466/64 logo into the concert. It was a big deal for me, as I had been told that my photo of Mandela's open palm would represent his call to free the world from HIV and AIDS.

One thing I hadn't experienced before were the larger-than-life managers and agents that accompanied these various rock stars. I was enthralled by it all. There was so much energy in the room that morning. It was fascinating to listen to these well-known individuals speaking to or about other famous people and places.

I wanted go about my work quietly, to capture every moment. The last thing I wanted to do was to knock a musician over or trip on the hundreds of wires running along the floor.

The director of the concert, whom I had only met once before, stood up and welcomed everyone. Various other people addressed the artists. I had begun to relax a bit, and was moving around doing my own thing. The director returned to the podium, but this time he spoke in a manner that commanded attention. Everyone stopped talking and looked at him in anticipation.

There are only a few moments in my life when I've been truly shocked. This was one of them. The director proceeded to introduce "a young man standing in the corner". With his right hand, he pointed directly at me.

"Ladies and Gentlemen, you may have seen this young chap walking around with his camera and I know many of you already know who he is, but it is my pleasure to let you all know that Matthew Willman is the photographer who took this amazing and evocative photograph of Nelson Mandela, which he has kindly allowed the 466/64 campaign to use as its logo and brand. Matthew, we thank you for your talent and commitment and we'd all like to take this opportunity to thank you collectively."

I could do nothing except stand in my corner, holding my camera, looking out at the multitude of people applauding me. Some were standing, a few whistled, others kept on clapping with the biggest smiles on their faces. I had been hurt a year earlier when I learnt that the Nelson Mandela Foundation had announced my photo as Mandela's choice without inviting me to attend the unveiling. But now, incredibly, if only for a few moments, some of the biggest names in the entertainment industry were honouring me.

So it was that on perhaps the very last day that Mandela ever came to his office at the Mandela Foundation, I was called to come up from Durban for a photoshoot. I had an idea what it was about. I was told it would only be me, Zelda la Grange and Verne Harris with Madiba.

It was a beautiful morning. The offices of the Foundation were quiet, people getting on with their work. Madiba slipped in quietly through the back entrance to his office. I don't recall there being any guests on this occasion. I was waiting in the lounge area immediately outside his office. Zelda was in good spirits and she invited me in. We all chatted for a bit. I completed the first part of the shoot and Verne, with a broad smile on his face, invited Madiba to raise his arm. I looked on in disbelief as Madiba lifted his arm. His fingers came together and, still kneeling on the floor, I looked up and there it was. After so many years of asking and worrying, Madiba finally allowed me to capture the image that would cement so many years of hard work. I finally got to do the portrait study of Mandela's 'Amandla Fist'.

Today, that large portrait is the focal piece of my photographic collection on Mandela. Few images in the world demand as much respect. In its symbolism and collective meaning, it stands as a testimony to all those around the world who are oppressed.

....

CHAPTER 16

WHERE DANCERS MOVE

*If you love an artist, keep your distance, for if you get too
close they may ruin the pantomime.*

Somewhere along the north end of Richmond Park in South-West London is a sign post with an arrow, reading simply: 'White Lodge'. It points down a long road, towards a thicket of trees. If you venture in you will discover that the road is flanked by two signs reading: "Private Road. No Thoroughfare'.

I had left the apartment before dawn to catch the south-west train to Richmond. From there, I made the long walk from the station up to the old village and the large public entrance into Richmond Park.

I had managed to save money for a flight to London and had spent a few days sleeping on the floor of a friend's tiny apartment near Wimbledon. I didn't have money to catch a tax. With time on my side, I walked the last five kilometres through Richmond

Park, across the dew-soaked common, along the oak-lined lane that brought me to the gates of the Royal Ballet School.

Even after all the walking and train journeys, I had arrived early. I left the road and wandered off into the forest adjoining the Ballet School, seeking images and scenes worth photographing.

I had passed a few deer along the road earlier, but my attempts to get close enough for a photo had simply chased them away. I discovered a huge oak tree that had fallen in the forest, exposing an intricate network of roots, which I thought would make an interesting study. It was a grave error. In my fresh pair of jeans, clean shoes and smart jacket, I stumbled and found myself wedged in a hole between roots and the very muddy ground. All manner of words and foul expressions ensued. Armed with only a few tissues and a bottle of water, I tidied myself up as best I could and presented myself at the front entrance to the Royal Ballet School. My arrival was not quite as I had imagined it.

I was greeted by a woman who leaned over her reception desk, peered over her half-moon glasses, and gave me what appeared to be a very disapproving once over. She then proceeded to enquire whom I wished to see. Trying to relax, I apologised for my appearance and explained that it was a long way from Africa and that I had fallen in a hole along the way.

The receptionist laughed, which helped me to relax.

Apart from the deathly silence in the reception hall, I could hear a distant piano playing and a teacher calling out over the music. It was hard to believe that after so many years of dancing on old melamine floors in South African schools, I found myself standing in White Lodge, the Royal Ballet School's Lower House (11 – 16 year olds). For many years, whilst growing up and training as a dancer, I had been told of a wondrous place in England where some of the finest ballet dancers in the world trained. Perhaps if we worked hard enough, we too would be chosen to dance there one day.

Principal Diane van Schoor interrupted my dreaming with a broad smile and a hand stretched out to greet me. The last time we had been in the same room was when she had examined me; then I had been a 16-year old dancer in a studio in Durban, South Africa. Between my dreams of the Royal Ballet School and my memories of my past life as a student of dance, it was all a bit surreal.

I had come to White Lodge to spend a few days photographing the school, in the hope of having my work published back in South Africa. After a long interrogation by the principal to ensure that I understood the rules of the ballet school, we made our way through to the staff room. The school bell had sounded and by the time we entered the staff room, the dance teachers and academic staff were already there enjoying their mid-morning tea break. Principal van Schoor called everyone to attention to formally introduce me, and to explain that I would be moving about the school, capturing images. With a smile on her face, she delighted everyone with the anecdote that she had personally adjudicated me for my Intermediate Level Exam in South Africa and awarded me a "Highly Commended" grade. The teachers all nodded in approval.

I interrupted.

"Sorry, Ma'am, but you awarded me Honours for my Intermediate Exam."

There was deathly silence. I am sure Principal van Schoor was unused to being corrected mid-sentence. However, I felt that there was a vast difference between being 'Highly Commended' and receiving 'Honours,' and I needed these highly qualified staff to recognise that I knew what I was doing.

Principal van Schoor simply smiled and said,

"Oh, I must have been having a really good day."

The staff all laughed; the introduction was over and everyone went back to their tea-time conversations.

Eager to change the topic, I commented on the room and its high ceilings. I discovered later that Vice-Admiral, Lord Horatio Nelson had stood in this same room to explain and expand his plans for the Battle of Trafalgar. I learnt too that White Lodge was the birthplace of King Edward VIII, and the residence of Queen Mary. Aside from ballet, a great deal of other history had occurred within these walls.

Sadly, pursuing a career in dance in South Africa has become increasingly challenging. A large section of South African society has never truly embraced ballet. Dancers earn meagre wages, and those who desire to work as company dancers tend to leave the country to pursue their careers abroad. As a boy growing up in South Africa, I was isolated, not only from society, but also within the dancing fraternity. There were so few male dancers that during all my training, I never once did a class with another male dancer. Principal van Schoor understood this. Soon after the tea break, she said there was something she wanted to show me.

I followed behind, her high-heeled shoes clattering down the narrow passageways. We stopped in front of one of the studio doors. I could hear a piano playing on the other side and the voice of a teacher calling out instructions to the dancers. Before opening the door, Principal van Schoor looked at me with a big smile, saying that this class was her pride and joy and that she was sure I would appreciate this great achievement. The door swung open, the pianist stopped playing and we entered a ballet class of eighteen young male dancers, each wearing their traditional black tights with white shirts. In unison, they all came to the centre of the dance hall and offered a greeting with a side step and a lowered head.

Principal van Schoor applauded them all and thanked them before returning them to the barre to continue training.

I was amazed. My whole life I had been alone in this experience and yet here in front of me was an entire class consisting exclusively of boys. It was astonishing. I understood now why Principal van Schoor was so proud. This level of achievement for male dancers is celebrated at the Royal Ballet School. The boys have a sense of pride in their work and this has become an important part of the success of the school.

With a polite turn, Principal van Schoor excused herself, invited me to visit her office whenever I passed by and left me standing alone, holding a camera in an entirely new and foreign environment. I had no idea where to even begin.

The commitment, training and sheer talent of these teenage boys certainly paid off. Six years later, I found myself photographing at the Vienna State Ballet in Austria, perhaps one of Europe's most celebrated ballet companies. What a privilege it was to shake the hands of a few of those young men now dancing as demi-soloists or soloists at the company. It was tremendous to see how strong and confident they had become.

For many years, I have worked on building a portfolio of artistic dance photographs that capture the intense artistry and ability of dancers from around the world. My goal has been to photograph dancers in an environment away from any theatre or dance studio. It has been my privilege to work with hundreds of dancers who strive every day to be seen, to perform and to pursue the dream of working professionally.

My biggest challenge has been to plan the images without having seen the locations. I cannot dictate the weather or who will be present while I am doing the shoot. This has been one of the largest personal projects I have undertaken, and has demanded everything of me. Every shoot stretches my imagination, pushing me to bring together the elements of lighting, location and composition to achieve images that are more than just proficient photographs. The images need to stimulate the viewers' imagination, capture a moment in time and be able to stand on their own as photographic art.

The dancers themselves are to be applauded for the images we have created. Not one has ever backed down from a challenge or failed to show up. They have never complained that my choreography doesn't work or that I was demanding too much. As artists committed to their craft, they strive to give their all and to extend themselves for the camera. Every shoot leaves me with a sense of awe and a responsibility to honour their talent and ability through capturing images that celebrate such beauty.

In New York City, I had gathered twenty dancers to work with. Over a two-week period, I traversed the city, working in subways and parks, at street crossings, bridges and buildings. Once a dancer was committed, a date was set. I'd choose and plan the location weeks in advance, using Google street view. I'd arrive ahead of our agreed meeting time to scour the location and work out the best angles for photographs. I'm acutely aware that the dancers I work with are professionals. They have a limited amount of energy and it would be wrong of me to make them repeat challenging movements that could potentially hurt them. As a former dancer, the whole process of photographing dancers is a marriage of my two great passions. Once I've choreographed a movement, I develop a sixth sense, an ability to capture it at its fullest extent or most creative moment. With the concept established, things quickly fall into place. I know what I'm looking for, so when the magic happens, I capture that split second. The dancers appreciate the fact that my shoots don't drag on and that they aren't required to repeat jumps over and over.

I won't lie; some days absolutely everything goes wrong. New York was having an intense heatwave in August that year. It became impossible to shoot in the heat. It was so bad that New Yorkers were fainting on the sidewalk. Wherever I walked, there were ambulances rushing to assist people. The subways were unbearable. I came across four women sitting in bikinis on a subway bench, protesting the lack of air-conditioning provided by the NYC Metro. What I love about New York is how proactive its citizens are in standing up for their rights and what they expect of their government. Yet even in that unbearable heat, every dancer arrived, none of them complained, and every one of them gave me powerful, transcendent images.

Dancers are fascinating people. I'm always intrigued by their artistry, how they see the world and what makes them tick. Most of my shoots have been outdoors and it has been wonderful to observe how each dancer has taken ownership of the space around them. I'm always concerned about them being in very public spaces, wearing tight clothing which may be revealing. I remember once meeting a young male dancer from the Cincinnati Ballet Company. Before going out into the streets of the city, I asked him if he wanted to 'cover up' until we reached the location. He politely declined and we set off, walking down the main street, me carrying my camera and him following, wearing nothing but the tightest hot pants and a pair of ballet shoes. Male dancers can often present themselves as passive or effeminate, but when they open up and express themselves for the camera, what they have to give is phenomenally powerful and exhibits extraordinary strength.

Throughout my career, I have believed in the marriage of dance and photography. The two are made for each other. Richard Avedon, the legendary American photographer from New York, believed this too. It can be clearly seen in his work with the Russian ballet dancer, Rudolph Nureyev. The two art forms speak to each other. The work I have achieved with dance as a professional photographer has far surpassed and completely satisfied my own desire to be a professional dancer. Through photography, I've been able to complete my artistry. Dance is always with me, whether I'm working with rural African communities or photographing famous people. My natural desire to capture movement is an element of my work that is directly influenced by the many years I spent training as a dancer in South Africa.

The opportunity to work with some of the most recognised ballet companies in Europe and the USA fulfils only part of my purpose in working with dancers. Another part of me desires to work with lesser-known dancers, irrespective of their background or achievements. Dance is inherently elitist, so I try not to show that in my work. One way to remove institutionalised dance is to photograph a cross-section of dancers from many different backgrounds. If they can move, then I will be there to capture it. I look for a certain intimacy, an expression of their individual beauty that moves me personally. Some shoots take a while to get that one shot. You have to work your way through until the dancer reveals that one moment that brings it all together.

I still have much to achieve, but ballet and the world of dance is an area which I have the pleasure of stepping into and out of. I don't own it and the industry doesn't own me. My ability to walk away from it at any point allows me to keep my work fresh and vital.

CHAPTER 17

MADIKIZELA OF BIZANA

Our greatest understandings lie on the other side of fear.

Winnie Madikizela-Mandela is one of South Africa's most formidable women. She is perhaps one of the most enigmatic, secretive and intriguing people I have ever met.

Whilst working on Robben Island, I was invited by the Robben Island Museum to attend a National Women's Day event at the V&A Waterfront precinct in Cape Town. I was at home in Durban, preparing for my next stint on the island, when the news came through that Winnie Madikizela-Mandela was going to attend the event. I was both thrilled and nervous because I sought something more from her than a brief meet and greet. I wanted her to sign a controversial photo taken by someone who had been stationed with the military in Soweto during the 1980s. The photo was taken from undisclosed photographic recordings commissioned by the military. They had attempted to document what was occurring during those days of unrest and strife in the townships.

The image depicted Winnie Mandela standing outside her tiny house in Vilakazi Street, Soweto welcoming some guests. The story went that the government had set up a hideout across the road to photograph Winnie Mandela's movements, who she met with and indeed all that occurred there.

I returned to Cape Town with the print, intent on getting Winnie Madikizela-Mandela to sign it. I checked into my hotel and spent the evening mentally rehearsing how I would approach her, and what I would say to get her to sign the image. As the evening wore on, my fear and anxiety grew. I had no idea how she would react to the photo and whether or not it would upset her. I might even be followed back to the hotel. My mind was running wild. I became totally neurotic, and in the early hours of the morning, after wrestling with the issue, I scrambled out of bed, tore the print into tiny pieces and flushed the evidence down the toilet. Such was the level of anxiety that this woman triggered in me.

The event itself went off very well. However, to my disappointment, Winnie Madikizela-Mandela failed to arrive. Instead, I had the privilege of sitting with one of South Africa's true mothers, Nontsikelelo Albertina Sisulu, the wife of another legendary African statesman, Walter Sisulu. Her grace and natural mothering of so many women and children in South Africa is legendary. Her love and care for the children of Soweto, the destitute and those in need during apartheid endeared her to the people of South Africa. Winnie Mandela and Albertina Sisulu both lived in Soweto. Winnie Mandela had a high wall around her small house, but Albertina Sisulu, living only a few roads away, had only a low gate that was always open to people who came and went all day.

The truth is I had formed an image in my mind of who Winnie Madikizela-Mandela was. I had read the books and heard the controversial accounts of her infamous life. I had spoken to an array of people who both loved and loathed her. I genuinely feared her, but that was not going to stop me from doing my best to meet her. As with my efforts to bombard PW Botha with questions, I wanted the opportunity to compare the character and personality of this woman with what I had read in books, newspapers and seen on television.

It wasn't until many years later, whilst in the thick of my work with the Nelson Mandela Foundation, that I became friendly with the Mandela family. I had been going on about how much I would love to meet Winnie Madikizela-Mandela and that nothing I tried seemed to be working. To my surprise and without any fuss, I received an e-mail inviting me to join the Mandela family for a Sunday afternoon lunch at Zenani Mandela's house in Johannesburg. It was hard to believe. For years I'd been knocking on so many doors and now, with one invitation, there I was going for lunch not only with the Mandela family, but Winnie Madikizela-Mandela herself.

The following Sunday, I found myself standing in the kitchen, talking with Zenani. Joining us for lunch that day was an old friend of the family, Peter Magubane. Peter is one of South Africa's foremost anti-apartheid documentary photographers. He has amassed a remarkable collection of photographs spanning more than 60 years. I had studied Magubane's work during my tertiary studies in photography. It was extraordinary to find myself in a kitchen with him, hanging on his every word as we discussed photography and his life.

We hadn't been talking long, when a tall, well-dressed gentleman entered the room. He greeted everyone, looked me up and down and left. Once the bodyguard had completed his rounds, he radioed whoever was outside, and Winnie Madikizela-Mandela entered the front door. The grandchildren all lined up to greet their grandmother, followed by the adults. There I was, at the end of the line, staring at her and still trying to convince myself that it was really her. We greeted. It was formal, but lacked any tension. Winnie smiled and enquired who I belonged to in the family. Everyone laughed. I dared not follow as she passed through the house to the kitchen to chat with the women. We relocated to the lounge and waited to be called to the dining room for lunch.

Lunch was a lengthy, slow affair. No-one was in a hurry, and it was wonderful. Madiba did not join the family that day and Winnie was content in her role as head of the family. Apart from the questions I asked Peter Magubane about his work, the conversation that afternoon was light-hearted. Occasionally, it strayed to their work and endeavours as a prominent family, their travel plans or issues around their children.

I still hadn't had the opportunity to chat with Winnie, but a few family members knew that I was keen to talk to her and made sure that I was seated next to her when it came to pudding time. It really was so relaxed. Winnie appeared to notice that I was now sitting right next to her, but carried on as normal. Many of the family members left to watch television, leaving a few of us still talking around the table. I hardly said a word. I had given up on the idea of speaking to Winnie and was content simply to be there.

Maybe it was my silence that drew her attention. For the first time that afternoon, Winnie turned to me and asked what I did. I looked at Peter Magubane and said that I was a photographer, aspiring to be just like Mr Magubane. They all laughed. Winnie smiled. She asked who I was working for. I think that she was a little surprised when I said that I was commissioned by the Nelson

Mandela Foundation. I noticed how she took note of this. She didn't say anything but nodded.

Taking advantage of the silence, I stepped out into the void and looking straight at Winnie, I told her that I had followed her life through many books and television documentaries. She looked directly at me, as if reconsidering me in a new light. I looked down at my empty pudding bowl and then, without making eye contact, I said,

"Mrs Madikizela-Mandela, I may not understand your pain, but I do recognise it."

It was as if I'd let a moth out of my mouth. It fluttered around the minds of everyone at the table. Immediately, the mood changed. I think everyone was keen to hear what her reply would be. Winnie moved her hand and placed it on my forearm, and began to speak in a low tone, choosing her words carefully.

"My child, you have no idea the pain I have been through. But I thank you for what you have said. You don't know my pain, but thank you for your words."

I was stunned. It was as if a veil had been lifted. Her words allowed everyone to relax, but they also allowed everyone to reflect on what had been said. I didn't stop there. I expressed my desire to take a few photographs of her before she left, if she was willing.

Winnie smiled and taking my hand she said, "For you, yes, of course."

I hadn't expected it to be so easy. Winnie moved her chair back and asked where I would like to shoot. Peter Magubane suddenly jumped up, becoming very excited, declaring that he would direct the photoshoot. It was crazy; the whole family got in on the occasion. I just kept laughing. We chatted away as we moved towards the lounge. I chose the spot and explained to Peter the look and feel I wanted. He agreed and then proceeded to place Winnie, careful to allow the afternoon light to fall beautifully across her face. It was too easy; it was a very precious time. With complete obedience to Peter Magubane, Winnie allowed herself to be moved around. He was very gentle but firm in his effort to get some special shots. The family laughed and joked, pretending they would make better models. Just as I was finishing up, I asked for one more photo. I asked if Winnie would allow me to photograph her hands. Winnie agreed and with care and attention to detail, I squeezed off a few photographs of her hands. I felt that, together with the portrait, they would complete my experience of Winnie Madikizela-Mandela.

I was planning to slip away, but Winnie asked for a pen and paper, saying she wanted to write me a note. Zenani, her daughter found a pen and paper in a drawer and politely gave them to her mother.

Dear Matthew,

Meeting honest young people like you makes me feel the struggle was worthwhile. I know now that the freedom we fought so hard for will be protected.

You will lead this country one day. Remember our children who gave up their lives for it in 1976. We owe it to you, the youth that we are free!

Amandla!

All power to the people,

Winnie Mandela

As she stood up, Winnie reached out and gave me a big hug. The family moved into another room and I sat there trying to digest what had just happened.

In the years that followed, I met Mrs Madikizela-Mandela at various luncheons and at the Nelson Mandela Foundation. It was always the same. Winnie would come up to me, give me a big hug and ask how her favourite photographer was. I'd smile and look at the ground, saying I was well. It was a little unnerving to receive so much attention from someone I had once feared so much.

Nelson Mandela and many other prominent people in South Africa will be remembered for the roles they played in the history of our country. I have been privileged to have had many personal glimpses into a number of their lives. I will remember those who crossed my path as I experienced them. The public will never know how doting Winnie Mandela was, in looking after her close friends. I cannot comment on or condone events outside my personal encounters. Sometimes this creates an inner conflict between my head and my heart. I have no illusions about any of the people I have engaged with.

I'm reminded of a story I came across whilst photographing on the Cape Flats in South Africa's Western Cape Province. The flats have been ravaged by the effects of drugs, gangsters and poverty. During my time there, I met and spoke with a social worker who was anxious to communicate that sometimes it is love and the simplest of actions that has the greatest impact.

Taking me by the hand, she walked me out into the middle of an open field. She pointed out that for years this field had been a no-man's land in the turf wars between two rival gangs. People had often been shot and killed while walking through here, simply going about their daily lives. This immediately made me uncomfortable.

In the middle of the field was a long, brick wall. It was painted white and a huge red heart had been painted on each side. The wall had been there a while but it was still in excellent condition. The social worker explained that she had built the wall and then painted it as I saw it. Surrounded by the decay of poverty, with houses and flats covered in graffiti, I was amazed that this one wall had not been vandalised.

The social worker smiled and said that years ago, when the wall was built, word had been sent out that it was a safe place for children to come and play. The gangs were told that they had no right to destroy this tiny place of hope and love. Not once has anyone taken aim at or tried to destroy the wall, despite gang wars and it still remains free of graffiti.

I looked at the social worker in total disbelief. She smiled then laughed.

"Matthew, can you see now that no matter how evil you are, or how powerful you think you are, even the worst person in the world knows how to love and knows what is good?"

I smiled. I understood for the first time that without words or any significant influence to overcome the scourge of drug wars on the Cape Flats, this young woman had shown that love conquers all.

···

CHAPTER 18

LITTLE BIRD

A true friend brings out the best in you.

If you drive through the trading post town of Lusikisiki and carry on down towards the coast, you drive through beautiful, landscaped tea plantations, before winding down through an indigenous coastal dune forest that opens onto an intimate estuary. The waves of the Indian Ocean crash along the endless, almost uninhabited beaches of the former Transkei coastline.

For centuries, the local Pondo have made their home up on the hills overlooking this remarkable coastline. Nestled along the estuary is a rustic log cabin hotel, so perfectly situated that it creates hardly any interference on this primitive, wild shoreline.

Mbotyi Lodge became our home for the week. Each day, at the crack of dawn, our group would travel out to engage with various communities in and around Pondoland. At night, we returned to this oasis tired, hungry and in need of a quiet spot to put our feet up, recount the events of the day, drink in hand, whilst listening to the crashing waves somewhere out in the inky darkness.

The hotel was almost empty. We hardly saw anyone else, so our small group of seven tended to take over the place in the evenings. We laughed and joked and since we all came from diverse backgrounds, took the time to learn about each other.

I loved being out in a faraway place, working as a team, experiencing new things each day. It was hard to believe that before becoming a documentary photographer I had been a completely different person, training for hours each day as an aspiring ballet dancer, aiming to achieve the highest standards of Cecchetti Ballet. Yet, here I was working at the coal face with communities in dire need of support, ravaged by the effects of HIV and AIDS, tuberculosis, poverty – communities fighting daily for survival. This was my life and yet ballet, although many worlds away, was with me even in this new world that I had created for myself.

This assignment was a little different. Our group had the rare opportunity to work with a woman who had been named as 'the greatest soul singer alive' and rated amongst the top 100 singers of all time, Annie Lennox.

We had met by absolute chance. I had been summoned to the Mandela Foundation for a shoot with Madiba. In preparing for Madiba's arrival, I kept walking past a small group of people, two women and two men. My defence for not recognising Annie is that I was focussed on making sure I was ready for Madiba. When I finally had a moment to sit in the lounge, I introduced myself. I realised that the two women were not South African and I wanted to share with them a little more about Madiba.

Mandela arrived and I left in a hurry, wishing them well, doubting that I would ever see them again. I did my brief shoot with Madiba, and after sorting out the images, I returned to discover the small group still there. Whilst I had been working on the images, they had gone to say a quick hello to Madiba. I never concerned myself unduly with who came to see Madiba. So many people of diverse nationalities and backgrounds passed through the doors. It wasn't always the rich and famous. Besides, I was generally focussed on the job at hand.

Since we were all leaving, I suggested I walk them out. We simply picked up and carried on the conversation where we had left off about an hour earlier. I was amazed at how interested this small group was in South Africa. Their questions were well thought out and relevant to what was occurring in the country at the time. I was very impressed. I thanked them for chatting, shook their hands and waited as they climbed into their car and off they went. Not five seconds later the car reversed, then stopped. One of the women jumped out and came back over to me. I thought she had forgotten something, so I was quick to ask if everything was okay.

In a clearly British accent, she asked if I had any idea who the other woman in her car was. I shook my head, embarrassed that I didn't know. She smiled and said, "That's quite alright," and proceeded to ask a question of her own.

"I know this sounds very weird and my friend in the car has never done anything like this before, which makes me nervous, but we were wondering what you were doing for the next two weeks?"

I told her I lived 600km south of Johannesburg and was about to drive home. I wasn't sure what the week ahead contained.

With that, this short, British-accented woman asked if I would like to join the four of them for a week in the Eastern Cape and then in Cape Town, as their photographer. They were meeting two other friends there the following day and they had space for a seventh person. I didn't really know them, but I loved the

Eastern Cape and they looked harmless enough. Besides, Mandela had allowed them to come and visit him. I needed no further encouragement.

"Sure, that would be great, thank you!"

We swapped e-mail addresses and I was told to be at the airport at 4am the next morning for a flight down to Umtata. Only then did I ask who the other woman was.

"I'm glad you asked, it's Annie Lennox, you know, the singer ..."

We shook hands, she climbed back into the car and they were off ...

As shocked as I was at what had just happened, the privilege of working with Annie Lennox was not the first thing going through my mind at that particular moment. Don't get me wrong, I was ecstatic, but I was more concerned that I didn't have any clothes to wear. This had started out as a one day shoot. I spent the rest of the day buying a few cheap clothes and rearranging my somewhat relaxed schedule.

The next morning, I arrived at the airport and there they were, true to their word: Annie Lennox, her personal assistant and the two men from the day before, her bodyguards whilst she was travelling in South Africa. We introduced ourselves more formally and Annie said how wonderful it was that I would consider traveling with them for the next two weeks. She gave me a big hug and just like that, we were all friends. 'Friends' is a very loose term. I later found out that personal assistants don't really like newbies, especially ones like me, who Annie had taken a liking to. But we kept a cordial relationship and only bumped heads a few times. All part of the game, I guess.

From that day forward, Annie and I have formed a very special friendship. As I have advanced on to new challenges and aspects of my work, we have kept in contact via e-mail, telephone calls, dinners in London, Johannesburg or Cape Town, and the odd text message here and there. We even undertook a spur-of-the-moment road trip together.

Waving goodbye to her husband, Annie and I set off to explore interesting places around the Western Cape Province for a few days. Picture two wired individuals, not afraid to discuss any subject, express any opinion or challenge any point of view, together in a car, zooting about enjoying being out and about. It was easy to forget who I was driving around with as we meandered from town to town, stopping in at coffee shops or mulling around old book stores and quaint side-street shops. There were some awkward moments when people recognised her, but we didn't experience any rudeness or threatening situations. One avid fan complimented Annie on her fine son, whilst looking directly at me. We both laughed, Annie smiled but didn't correct him. In all the time we have known one another, I have taken only two photographs of us together. Both were unplanned and feature grins far too cheesy for public viewing.

I've learnt a tremendous amount from Annie. Initially, I was a complete novice at working around a person who is both relaxed and not at all egocentric, and yet has a public image to maintain. I realised very quickly that Annie was required to balance her dual roles of being an international rock star with legions of followers, and her role as a UN Ambassador for HIV and AIDS and other international charities. I had to sharpen up very quickly when photographing her. I had to ensure I was respectful of this person and what she represented, both inside and outside of this massive public persona.

When working with her in my capacity as a photographer, the focus was on the immediate issues at hand. The going was tough; it was hot, and the conditions we encountered demanded restraint, empathy and focus in order to be of service and value to those we were engaging with. But in the evening, guided by Annie, we all let our hair down. I loved the evenings; it was our time to truly relax and learn about each other.

I'll never forget one evening – we were all laughing and talking, when Annie suddenly turned to me, eager to ask what she and the others deemed was a very personal question. I had said hardly anything about my personal life, careful not to be perceived as too familiar. So I agreed to do my best to answer her question. Everyone had stopped talking and watched the scene play out.

"I've been watching you, you move so beautifully; I wanted to know, are you a dancer?"

Aah, man, was it that noticeable? I laughed suddenly, feeling very exposed.

"Yes, I danced for 18 years as a ballet dancer …" There was a pensive moment of silence. I wasn't sure what was coming next. Then the whole group packed up laughing. Annie was thrilled. She turned to the others pointing and beamed.

"See I told you! I just knew he was a dancer! He moves so beautifully, as if he understands the space around him!" She gave me big hug and then, commanding everyone's attention, asked if I would teach her a few steps of ballet.

I flopped back into my chair, unsure what was happening. We were in the hotel lounge! I looked up over the sofas. Nobody else was in the immediate vicinity, so I calmly stood up, moved aside a few chairs and told everyone to stand up and find a space, as I was about to teach them all the eight basic body positions of Cecchetti ballet.

What followed next makes me laugh even today. With shrieks of laughter, interspersed with a few bottles of red wine and a whole lot of crazy ballet positions, together we created a treasured memory; even the body guards gave it a go. Never in my wildest imagination, would I have pictured myself in a rustic hotel, on the rugged Pondoland coastline, teaching ballet to Annie Lennox!

Gradually, calm descended. A warm breeze filtered in through the open doors, the night air thick and heavy with the salty sea air. As happened on most evenings, we ended simply sitting quietly, lost in our own worlds. One by one, people moved off to their rooms. Annie curled up on the sofa next to me and began to sing. One of my most treasured memories during those precious few days, far away from the world, was the privilege of that moment with Annie singing old, forgotten songs that told of love and the heart's desire.

Over the years, I have experienced the privilege of photographing and interacting with some truly inspiring and hard-working individuals, whose talent and sheer determination has afforded them global recognition. At such times, surrounded by some of the best photographers in the world, I feel the weight of responsibility and a sense of inadequacy. For I realise how flawed my photography is. I am by no means one of the best photographers in the world. There are others who would be much better, more adept and relaxed photographing these important people. I merely used my camera to take me out there, and whilst out there captured moments that, with enough time, will grow in value.

Occasionally, I'm asked who I would like to photograph. I always reply, "Her Majesty Queen Elizabeth II". Most photographers would readily agree. Yet I feel deep down inside, that the task would prove too mammoth for me. Picturing the stress and formality leaves me with rocks in my stomach. I've seen YouTube videos of Annie Leibovitz working with the Queen, and I can read between the lines how stressful it all is. Even Leibovitz made mistakes during that shoot. I'd never forgive myself if I were to make some fundamental mistake. The stratosphere that the Queen exists in is too much for me. With Mandela it was different; I was given the leeway to interpret him as I saw fit. I hardly ever look through the images I captured during my many years of work with Mandela. I cringe at how often I missed a shot or could have done better. I don't deny that I did create some superb images, but I'm very conscious of where I was at that time in my life and it leaves me feeling a little unsettled. Can you imagine the ranks of personnel that one would have to pass through in order to work with the Queen? Only those who have worked at this level can appreciate this.

The point I'm making is that the images I did get right are made more precious by the fact that they are selected from amongst hundreds of mistakes and sub-standard photographs. I used to get myself into serious knots, knowing that I needed to present the Mandela Foundation with a portfolio of superb images from each shoot. If I didn't, I would be out in the cold, looking in. Some days, I truly believe that no-one took the time to go through the images presented, or they mercifully kept their mouths shut, or selected one or two from the range I gave them. Perhaps it is for this very reason that throughout my career, I have kept a very sober or considered attitude about my images and the opportunities I have had.

I liken it to diamond mining. You dig like crazy, going through miles of solid rock and only every now and then do you haul out a tiny diamond. In my work for charities in Southern and Eastern Africa, I shot thousands of images, hoping and praying that they would discover a few good enough to employ me again. I hoped and prayed that the images I saw in my mind were translating themselves from my imagination into the final product. I was always amazed when I saw one of my images on television or in a newspaper and realised that it had become a success and was being used around the world to promote a certain cause. Like tiny seeds, they grew and took on a life of their own.

One of Annie's many strong points is that she loves to engage with people. For a person who is often in the limelight, I'm always amazed at her ability to listen. It's beautiful. I have often gone off on a conversational tangent, only to realise when I 'resurface', that she was still sitting there patiently listening.

I have always been impressed by her interest in South Africa. She engages not at a surface level, but deeply, on a broad range of topics that many South Africans wouldn't even understand or know about.

While traveling around Cape Town, I got a bee in my bonnet that there were a few people Annie needed meet. I was sure she would be keen to speak to them.

So, we hopped into the car and made our way through the city to Milnerton, a suburb up the coast from Cape Town, to spend an hour with South Africa's very own Archbishop Desmond Tutu. I had phoned Tutu's assistant the day before. Fortunately, the Archbishop had an hour free in the morning and was very keen to meet with Annie. All I had to do was arrive with Annie and leave them to it. We arrived and all the staff at his Foundation were lined up, smiling and taking pictures. Annie greeted each one and posed for photos, enjoying the moment. Then we heard the exuberant voice of the Archbishop coming down the hall. He made a joke, reminding all that she was in fact there to see him, then took her by the hand and went through to a room to chat. I was fascinated at how polite they were with each other. Annie had as many questions for the Archbishop as he had for her. Out of the blue, he insisted that she sing him a song. Annie tried to laugh it off, but he insisted. He clasped his hands together, closed his eyes and as if in deep prayer, he smiled whilst Annie sang him a song. Tutu gave out a cry of joy and satisfaction.

"How wonderful, how wonderful!" he repeated over and over again. Annie went bright pink with embarrassment. I remember sitting in the car on our way back to Cape Town, laughing as we playfully impersonated Tutu asking Annie to sing.

The other person we visited was less playful. Then mayor of Cape Town, Helen Zille was also the leader of the Democratic Alliance, the official opposition party in South Africa. From the outset, the tone of conversation was very different to that with Tutu. We found ourselves on the top floor of the Civic Centre, in the board room of the Mayoral Chambers. There were three people in that boardroom that day: me, Annie and Mayor Zille. I made sure to stay out of the way. They sat talking at one end of the boardroom table, while I sat at the other end. It was entertaining listening to them talk. They had strong opinions on a variety of topics, but neither allowed their differences to supersede their recognition of the other's commitment to the challenges faced by the communities in which they worked. The car trip home was quiet, broken only by Annie expressing a final opinion on an issue she had spoken about with Zille. We all abstained from comment.

I remember driving back from Stellenbosch late one evening. Annie and I had spent the day traveling to Paarl, to visit the prison house where Nelson Mandela had lived for the last 18 months of his incarceration. It was from this house that Nelson Mandela had walked to freedom on the 11th of February 1990. I had worked at the house many times, documenting it for the Nelson Mandela Foundation, so it was relatively easy to get access for a private visit from the Victor Verster Prison authorities. The whole experience had been very moving and emotionally draining. Annie had listened to all the stories that I and the Chief Warden had told. It was fascinating to watch Annie move from room to room absorbing all the stories. Every now and then, I'd notice how she would gently touch something in the house, a light switch or bathroom tap. Everything had meaning and through these simple everyday objects, Annie was able to connect with the history and humanity of this man, Nelson Mandela. It was difficult to pull ourselves away from the house. We wanted to linger, walk around, trying to imagine what it must have been like all those years ago for someone to have endured so much pain, to walk out this prison house ready to change an entire nation forever. We left the house late in the afternoon. We grabbed some coffee and made our way through Helshoogte Pass down into the town of Stellenbosch. We passed through the town and headed back to Cape Town. For a long time, neither of us said anything to each other. A few times, one of us would start a conversation or pose a question that would fade away as we both reflected on what we had experienced that day.

With Stellenbosch behind us, we could see the lights of Cape Town shimmering in the distance. Annie had pushed her seat back, her arm was up against the window and her face was turned, looking out the window, staring at the passing vineyards, farms and general traffic. I was glad for the peace. I was trying to calculate how I was going to orchestrate the next two days. I needed to drop Annie off at her home, head back out to Paarl to hopefully get in a few hours of sleep, before leaving at 3am to drive the 1 600km back home to Durban. Annie must have been reading my mind at that moment. For the first time in a while, she turned her head and asked if I was up for dinner at a superb little restaurant she knew near her place. I had spent the past half hour calculating the sleep I needed in order to drive 18 hours back to Durban the next day. I didn't hesitate: *Yes, of course, what a great idea, dinner sounded perfect. Who needed sleep, let's carry on the party.*

Unlike Archbishop Tutu, I've never asked Annie to sing. I've always felt the privilege belonged to those who paid money to see her perform. As the city lights drew nearer, we both fell silent again, listening to the hum of the car engine and the tyres on the tar road. It's very difficult to try to express what happened next. It was as if I had turned on the radio but instead of music coming through the cars speakers, the music emanated from the heart and soul of Annie Lennox sitting right beside me, staring out at the passing cars. Her hauntingly beautiful voice filled the tiny enclosed bubble of my car. Only I could hear it. It was a gift I certainly didn't deserve. Maybe it was for herself, a way to unwind, to get in touch, to centre herself, and I just happened to be the incredibly lucky guy who was driving her home that evening. What I do know, is that it was incredibly real and personal. I didn't dare look across at her. Instead of my usual determination to sit at the maximum road speed allowed, I held back on the throttle, slowing the car to a comfortable speed. The lights of the Cape Town city bowl flickered and danced in myriad colours as we made our way around the mountain. There have been some beautiful moments in my life, but few, if any, will ever come close to that day in my car.

Dinner was spent laughing and regaling one another with stories. As much as I wanted things to go on and on, I eventually had to make the call to leave. The clock struck midnight and my perfect day was fast becoming a beautiful memory. I drove away that night, knowing that I had only three hours until I had to get up and head home. As I turned onto the N1 highway, heading back to Paarl, I smiled. I wouldn't have changed it for the world.

. . . .

CHAPTER 19

THE 42ND PRESIDENT

"Every time Nelson Mandela walks into a room, we all feel a little bigger; we all want to stand up, we all want to cheer, because we'd like to be him on our best day."
- U.S. President Bill Clinton, welcoming Nelson Mandela to the White House, 22 September 1998

July at the Nelson Mandela Foundation was always a special time. With Mandela's birthday on the 18th of July, a lot happened around that time. Not only were there birthday cakes galore, but it was a time that many personalities came by to wish Madiba a happy birthday.

One particular guest arrived with a little more pomp and ceremony than the others: former President of the United States, Bill Clinton. On three occasions, I had the pleasure of being invited to the Mandela Foundation to photograph President Clinton. The day would start with Madiba arriving at his usual time, around

10am. Spot on 11am the motorcade would roll through the gates of the Foundation and round to the rear of the building, where a private entrance gave President Clinton the privacy of greeting Madiba without the buzz of the media that followed him wherever he went.

I'd be lying if I said I wasn't excited. Living in Africa, the pull and fascination of America was huge. In those days, I had not visited America, so it was a big deal that I was meeting perhaps one of the most popular and successful American presidents of my lifetime.

The first taste of what was to come was the security detail. I had to submit a copy of my ID, get accreditation and have my name added to an approved list some weeks in advance, in order to even be allowed on the premises that day. Once inside the building, we were not allowed to leave. Hours before the president's arrival, Secret Service members walked around the Foundation offices, keeping an eye on everything that was happening. It was fascinating. I felt as if I was doing something wrong, just walking around performing my usual tasks. I always wondered how Mandela's own security detail managed to collaborate with them: two highly trained units, both working to protect their respective 'number one'.

Just as President Clinton arrived, I was ushered into Mandela's office. I greeted Madiba with a big smile. He replied with a nod and a wave of his hand. I backed away to assume my usual position, off to one side. The double doors to the private entrance swung open and Secret Service agents stepped into the office, followed a few seconds later by President Clinton.

I was standing just to the right of the door, so when President Clinton entered the room it was easy to get an idea of how tall he was. I was amazed at how commanding his presence was. I was trying to photograph his entrance whilst feeling a sense of awe. Right next to me, was this man whom I'd only ever seen on television, a man who at one time was considered the most influential and powerful man in the world. The realisation was incredibly sobering and daunting at the same time.

Only a few steps into the office, President Clinton stopped. It was only then that I noticed that he was holding a fine bone-china teacup and saucer. He hesitated very briefly. I was closest to him and he held out the cup and saucer towards me. Like a supremo, Zelda swooped in and took the china from him. President Clinton, arms open wide, greeted Madiba with a massive bear hug. It was wonderful to see two old friends greeting each other after some time apart. I was amazed at how careful and respectful President Clinton was around Madiba. The two of them shared a few pleasantries together and laughed about a few things I couldn't quite make out. Once the photographs had been taken, I moved out of the room into the lounge reserved for guests waiting to meet Madiba. A few minutes later, arm in arm, Nelson Mandela and President Clinton walked through the doors into the lounge area. We were joined by other photographers. At this point, I had no idea what was going on. Madiba sat in his usual blue wing-back chair, and one by one President Clinton's entourage were introduced. As this was occurring, Zelda glared at me and in her usual firm way told me to leave as I was no longer needed. Listening to the boss, I left. I was amazed at how long the queue was leading into the lounge, easily more than eighty people.

The whole event that day was a balancing act of security, protocol, media, guests, VIP guests and the entourages of these two famous leaders. I popped my head into the packed auditorium and was amazed to see many luminaries of South Africa's social circles and possibly the biggest press corps I had ever seen gathered in the auditorium.

President Clinton made his way through towards the auditorium first. Along with a few members of the Mandela Foundation, I had joined a queue to formally greet the president. When my turn came, we shook hands, but I stupidly broke protocol by patting the president on his shoulder as we greeted. It was a stupid thing to do. President Clinton was familiar with me, and he had greeted me with such warmth it was difficult not to give him some love back. My reaction was an authentic expression of respect. I like to believe President Clinton thought the same as he in turn did the same to me with his other hand. The moment was over in a flash before President Clinton moved onto the next person. Unfortunately, security agents had noticed my hand on the president's shoulder. They waited until President Clinton was further down the line before stepping into my face, telling me that if I ever touched the president like that again, they would remove me from his presence. Instead of being afraid and cowering in their overpowering presence, I let out a laugh and reminded them they were in Mandela's house and all of us were his welcomed guests. Without waiting for their response, I turned and headed back towards Mandela's office to assume my duties for the Nelson Mandela Foundation. Later that evening, at a private dinner at the Saxon Hotel, those same security guards were surprised to see me yet again with Mandela. We didn't say anything to each other. I had nothing to apologise for. Perhaps they would have preferred that I wasn't there.

Soon after President Clinton had made a tour to greet the staff of the Foundation, Mandela himself appeared and together they walked into the auditorium. I walked just in front of them snapping away. At the door to the auditorium, I slipped through, found my spot and then like the rest of those gathered, enjoyed the spectacle of the next hour.

I liken those days to a big production. My camera was my ticket to both the front row and backstage. I got to experience how the whole 'show' worked. Most 'public' days, when the Mandela Foundation was on show before the whole world, played out the same. Perhaps because the former President of the United States was the guest that day, tensions were higher and security tighter. What I know for certain, is that moving about amongst it all was terribly exciting.

Once the two former presidents had left the building to have lunch at Mandela's house, the whole mood changed; people relaxed to enjoy the Mandela Foundation's hospitality. The Foundation always laid on an impressive array of food and the regulars who attended functions made sure to stay. I enjoyed this part of the day the most. I got to interact with a cross-section of South African society. As always, I knew that within a day or two I would return home to my tiny world far away from the glitz and glamour of Johannesburg and the Nelson Mandela Foundation.

In the early days, my routine on returning home was always the same. On days when we finished late at the Foundation, I would arrive home around 9pm, having driven 600 kilometres. I would dump my bags on the kitchen counter and leave them there until the morning. I'd take a shower and try to mentally unpack what had happened that day. My mind was often in overdrive as I tried to piece together the day's unique events, comments and mental images of the pictures I'd taken. More than anything, I was trying to come to terms with this surreal life and my role in it.

The days that followed my exciting experiences at the Mandela Foundation were indeed the hardest. I'd bump into my neighbour in our block of flats. She would be none the wiser about my experience. She only asked why I'd left so early the day before and returned so late.

The reality was that I was depressed. I'd listen to stories of how my friends were getting on with their lives. Most were totally unconcerned or disinterested in anything happening outside their own immediate worlds. I certainly didn't hold this against them. Why should they be concerned or interested in what I was doing? I found myself caught up in a vortex between what was happening within my career and the everyday reality of my home community. I had no clients in Durban. Aspects of my career beyond the Mandela Foundation took me to other cities in South Africa and even further afield to England, America and Ethiopia – wherever!

After a few days, I'd get over my depression and focus on the next opportunity or adventure with my camera. I soon realised that these were 'bubbles' I stepped in and out of. They were not 'my reality'. I was only there to provide a service, to build my own portfolio and then to exit. I certainly was not friends with those I worked with. I performed my duty and left.

....

CHAPTER 20

A GIRL IN THE DESERT

I used to think only great adventurers discovered new horizons. It turns out every child longing for their dream is already there.

One of the boldest moves I ever made was to let go of security. It was simple. I knew that I had such seemingly insurmountable odds to overcome, that if the challenge wasn't scary enough, if at any point I felt safe and secure, I would be wasting my time.

The first time I drove to Cape Town to meet Archbishop Desmond Tutu was also the first time that I ever left home to travel across South Africa on my own. Cape Town was 1 600 kilometres away. I had two days to get there, so I simply climbed into my car and drove, without any plan of where I would end up the first night. By nightfall things weren't looking too good. I had romanticised the idea of heading out and laying my head wherever

I found myself at day's end. The reality was that when the time came to stop, I was in the middle of nowhere with nothing but scrubland bush, wire fences on either side of the road, sand and very large wide-open spaces beyond. There were things lurking out there that scared me to death.

That night I camped in my car, just off the main road. For the first time in my life, I had done something without considering the consequences of being so far from home that I couldn't turn around and go back. I found an old gravel road, cozied up to a big old tree, turned off the engine and sat there. For the first time in my life I knew what it was like to be alone. I was so afraid that something out there was waiting to attack me that I didn't even get out of the car to urinate. I filled an empty bottle and threw it out of the window. I was convinced I had landed myself in serious trouble. By the time I crawled over into the back seat to try to sleep, I was crying my eyes out. I had never felt so alone and so pathetic. All I could do was cry.

I was so overcome by emotional turmoil and how reckless I had been, that I convinced myself that at first light I would turn around and go home. I persuaded myself that the only security I needed at this point was the comfort and familiarity of my bedroom back home. I had explored how far I could stretch myself and discovered that I had gone too far. I had failed but at least no-one knew, so I would just go home and never pull this stunt again.

I blew my nose, calmed down a bit and lay back, looking up through the car window into the night skies. It was beautiful. Above me was the most immaculate array of heavenly stars. I found myself mesmerised with the enormity and splendour of looking up at what felt like the entire universe. I pulled my blanket right up under my chin and lay there in awe of the heavens that reigned over me. My fear subsided and I began to laugh. What I was doing was absolutely amazing. Here I was, somewhere out in the middle of the Karoo, no-one knew where I was, no-one could reach me and yet for the first time in my life I felt alive. I had conquered one of my biggest fears. Just at my point of terror, when I had decided that I had gone too far, I had taken a deep breath and realised what a privilege it was to be on an adventure. Out here on my own, reckoning with myself, discovering who I was, I was exactly where I wanted to be. There welled up inside me a primal urge to be wild and different. In a few moments, heart-wrenching tears gave way to such deep laughter, that tears of joy rolled down my face. I had driven over the hump in the road to discovery. I had broken through a massive barrier that night and instead of defining my boundary, I had in fact pushed it out even further.

Teddy Roosevelt once wrote:

"It is not the critic who counts; not the man who points out how the strong man stumbled, or where the doer of deeds could have done them better. The credit belongs to the man who is actually in the arena, whose face is marred by dust and sweat and blood; who strives valiantly ... who knows great enthusiasms, the great devotions; who spends himself in a worthy cause; who at the best knows, in the end the triumph of high achievement, and who, at the worst, if he fails, at least fails while daring greatly so that his place shall never be with those cold and timid souls who know neither victory nor defeat."

- Theodore Roosevelt, The Man in the Arena, from Citizenship In A Republic, 1910

I wanted to meet Nelson Mandela, but he certainly wasn't going to come looking for me. Neither was I ever going to discover a miraculous script for my life that would give me the confidence and security to go out into the big wide world. The first hurdle I had to overcome was to simply get up and go. The more you cast fear and insecurity aside, the stronger you become. It doesn't get any easier, you just grow stronger.

It was only in dealing with myself that I became aware of the world around me, where I began to discover the lives of others. The following story of an experience I had whilst out exploring, defines in its innocence who we are and how we connect with the world.

Huhudi Township is hot; in fact it's very hot. This huddle of corrugated tin shacks lies at the edge of the immense Kalahari Desert, which reaches up north into Botswana. The settlement is close to the town of Vryburg. Somehow, the population of shack dwellers eke out a living in a desert where it is over 50 degrees Celsius during the day and minus 5 degrees Celsius at night. These people of Khoi-San descent are remarkable in their ability to subsist in this inhospitable environment.

I had not intentionally travelled vast distances to photograph this particular township settlement. I merely stumbled upon it whilst exploring the area, trying to build up my documentary portfolio. I was looking for more than images. I was looking for stories.

One afternoon, I was walking with a group of school children along an old railway track heading towards town. I had been in the area a few days, exploring the local farms dotted around this vast open expanse of sand, rocks, desert grass and thorn bushes. I happened upon an old train station, next to a school carved out of the desert surrounds. School was out and kids were all moving in the general direction of their homes a few kilometres down the road in Huhudi township. I decided I'd join them and try to get a few good images. Being the only white guy around, I created some interest and was soon surrounded by noisy kids all wanting to touch me and tell me something in their local language. Apart from being the centre of attention, I wasn't capturing anything worthwhile. Having acknowledged to myself that I wasn't going to achieve much, I began to head back to my car. Unexpectedly, a young woman marched up to me. In simple English, she told me her name and that she had been to the Antarctic. I laughed in disbelief, and asked her to repeat what she had just said. Again she told me her name and repeated that she had been to the Antarctic.

"That's what I thought you said. Do you speak any more English?"

"Yes I do." Her stance became even more assertive.

"Really ... and when did you go to the Antarctic?"

"Two years ago." Her answer was quick and to the point.

"How old are you?"

"Twenty years."

"And you say you've been to the Antarctic?"

"Yes, I told you that already!"

I wasn't sure I could believe her. For all I knew, she had heard of about Antarctica in the classroom and thought it foreign enough to tell me she had been there. Perhaps she merely wanted some kind of reaction from me or to tease me in front of her friends. Behind her a group of girls giggled, which further added to my suspicions.

"Okay," I went on. "So, tell me, where did you say you had been again?" I looked at her sideways, pretending to fix something on my camera.

"Antarctica. Do you know where that is?"

I laughed again.

"I do, but do you?"

"Yes," she shot back, as if I'd offended her.

"Okay, I'm sorry. It's just that it's so hot here. We are out on the edge of the Kalahari Desert, five hundred kilometres from the nearest ocean. This area has a thousand years of history as a place of hunter gatherers (the Khoi-San) and you are telling me you've been to Antarctica? It's a little hard to believe." I wanted to test her further. "Okay, so where is the Antarctic exactly?"

Still feeling that she had to prove herself to me, she started to talk.

"We flew from Cape Town on Varig Airlines to Brazil, and then we connected on a smaller plane, down to Tierra del Fuego in Chile. From there we caught a boat that took us for five days till we landed on the first mainland of the Antarctic."

I was sold. I couldn't believe what she had said. She waited for me to respond. I couldn't, nothing came out.

"But how? Why? You're a poor girl from a township in a desert on the Botswana border. Do you even know what snow is?" My mind was racing at this point. "Okay, wait, start at the beginning. Have you ever seen the ocean before?"

"No, but it was so big."

"Okay, stop. Start again. How on earth did you even get to go to the Antarctic?"

"My grandmother lives in Soweto in Johannesburg. Every few months she sends me a copy of the latest *True Love* magazine (a popular magazine in South Africa). In one of those magazines, was a competition run by the loveLife Campaign (an HIV/AIDS awareness organisation). They were partnering with some international organisation to find a group of young adults and teenagers from around the world to travel to the Antarctic to clean it up, as a symbolic gesture to show how vulnerable our climate it. So I entered and won. We went for three months. It was the first time I saw snow. It was very cold!"

I couldn't believe what she was telling me. Here we were, miles away from anything that hinted at any opportunity in life. All around me, people were battling just to feed themselves or to pay for their children to go to primary school, let alone high school, and here was a girl with a life-changing story. A story that said there is always hope, anything is possible. Anything!

She continued.

"But it was so difficult. I was so homesick, seasick and airsick. I just wanted to die. I cried and cried. I didn't know anyone and we were always being told what to do. I was with other teenagers from around the world, but no-one could speak my language."

I stopped her again:

"I'm sorry, but I have to ask you something. How on earth did you manage to get over the cold and homesickness?"

She didn't answer at first. She looked out across the vast desert flats, focusing on some imaginary point on the oily horizon or perhaps even further away, somewhere deep within herself. She took a long time to reply, but eventually she took a deep breath and shared her story. What she said will stay with me for the rest of my life.

"You know," she began, "when I was homesick, I felt very far away from everything. It was so cold and there was ice everywhere. I couldn't call home or even write. But I tell you what I did. When it wasn't falling with the snow, I would go out with a spade, walk a bit and then I would begin to dig. I'd dig and dig and dig, until I hit the earth underneath. I'd make a hole in the soft snow and climb inside the hole, and in there I'd sit on the earth, even if it was only a few rocks. When I was in there, I knew I was home. I was touching the same earth that my family were touching back home. I knew that even under that big ocean and across this dry and barren desert, my family were going about their lives, touching the same earth that I was sitting on so far away. It was the only thing that gave me comfort."

I sat there lost in her story, something so foreign to me. I was intrigued that all she had to do to reach out and touch home was to touch the earth. She came from a people whose descendants reached back to the 'Bushmen', the hunter-gatherers of Africa. She understood the value of the life-giving earth beneath her feet. She had connected to her home by touching the earth. She had travelled beyond the south Atlantic Ocean, across the blisteringly hot, equally lifeless deserts of the northern Karoo to her home, a tiny tin hut in a township forgotten by the rest of the world,

I began my social and political awakening and development during a time in South Africa when the foundations of our new democracy were still being solidified. It was a time when South Africa both wept for its tragic past and advanced with determination towards its renewal. We were a people so resilient that we all moved forward, guided by our will to create a new nation under the leadership of Nelson Mandela.

Across South Africa, businesses and government were desperate to discover stories of reconciliation and hope, proof that change was not only something to be written about, but was actually occurring in the everyday lives of her people.

It was a challenging time. For the first time, different communities had to engage with each other, whether they liked it or not. In urban areas, this was easier to do, but out in the rural farmlands and places still entrenched in apartheid living, the voice of change was not even a whisper.

I've spent many days during the course of my career, wandering alone with my camera looking for images and stories. When I look back now, I'm awed at the determination I had to persevere until I got the shot. The more time I spent out there, the less I wanted to go home. It gave me a sense of purpose.

Sometimes, the isolation caught up with me, and I'd come across a situation that pulled at my heart strings and reminded me that I was human, with my own needs and desires.

A client had engaged me to spend a week in Kimberley, to photograph development projects they were funding on the outskirts of this mining town. I had been to Kimberley a few times over the years, so I knew my way around. My plane landed an hour or two before sunset, so before I checked into my hotel, I'd collect my hired car and head out into the surrounding desert. I loved the desert, especially in the late evenings when the sun had lost its heat and the colours of the desert were astounding. In my hired car, I would choose an old dusty road and then drive until I found a rocky hilltop or a large enough tree to climb, so that I could get a view out over the grasslands.

I didn't often come across many people out there, so when I started to head back to town in my car, I was surprised to see two people walking in the distance along the dusty road. At first I thought they must have been labourers on their way home from one of the farms. As I drew closer, I realised that I had happened upon something special. One of the men was an elderly black man; he walked along at a steady pace. Walking alongside him with a kind of spring in his step, was a young white boy, not more than twelve years old. I was fascinated. I stopped my car and for the next few minutes, enjoyed the privilege of sitting there, watching these two people making their way down the road towards an old farm gate. It seemed the young boy was telling some big story, as his hands were waving about and he laughed as he went along. The old man was more considered, but every now and then he would look at the boy and nod his head.

What I loved about this scene was that it was happening

regardless of my being there to witness it. I took a few photos with my telephoto lens that evening. It warmed my heart to witness that apartheid had not destroyed everything good about South Africa. Every time I see this image, I'm reminded that we can rebuild and that our challenges can be overcome, no matter how insurmountable they may be.

· ·

CHAPTER 21

WALKING WITH DINOSAURS

Anything is possible, even real dinosaurs.

Most photoshoots have a sense of purpose and gratification, but occasionally a shoot comes along that makes me want to go home the moment I've arrived. Never in my life have I been treated as badly or made to feel as insignificant as I was on the set of a British film production about dinosaurs. I was recruited through an agent in London, and I signed on because I felt that working on this film production offered something new and exciting.

I came on board as a stills photographer, capturing images of the locations for the production team. The images were sent off to London, where the digital team added in the dinosaurs. By the time I joined the production team in South Africa, they had already spent a substantial time shooting in some pretty harsh conditions, at various locations around the world. Everyone's nerves were frayed and most of the crew had lost interest. During those final two weeks of shooting, this surfaced in bad tempers, unpleasant remarks and general unfriendliness. That aside, I made good friends with the animatronics guys, a chirpy bunch who absolutely loved their craft. They had two, huge eighteen-wheeler trailers filled with props, puppets and a mind-boggling arsenal of wizardry, including smoke machines and stun bombs. It turned out that they were the same crew who had worked on the Harry Potter films, so I was dead keen to soak up this new experience.

The film crew had cordoned off a large area in the Umfolozi Game Reserve with one main gravel road running through the set, or so we thought! For much of the time, we simply sat around waiting to be called. I had 'moved in' with the animatronics guys and only ventured onto set when called by one of those irritating 'runners' wearing a headset, three cell phones and a clipboard. The first day was easy; the lighting was good and I was careful not to bother the producer or his minions, but on the second day and the three subsequent days, things just kept getting worse. It began to rain and it didn't let up. There was mud everywhere. The budgets were already over-stretched and completion dates were looming.

Fortunately, on the fifth day the clouds lifted, the rain stopped and everything came to life. The final scene to be filmed was a long shot where the camera panned into a valley, capturing a Tyrannosaurus Rex walking through the scrub and thorn trees. The animatronic puppeteers had built a life-sized head of this once fearsome beast. The rest of the body would be filled in during post-production using CG animation. All the puppeteer had to do was to make sure that the positioning of the head, its angle and height above the ground matched the movement of a T-Rex.

My job, while the cameramen and director filmed their scenes, was to find a spot far away from them and capture images of this

T-Rex walking in the bush against the African backdrop to create the mood. It was late in the evening, the lighting was perfect and things were going well. I was perched behind a tree about a hundred metres from where they were filming. I was so far out of the picture that I could move around getting my shots. All was going well until I heard, coming round the side of a hill, a tourist bus on an early evening game drive. Someone in security had failed to notice that there was a second gravel road that linked to the one we had been given permission to cordon off.

Hidden among the thorn trees, I watched as the tour-bus came closer. It had passed me and travelled about twenty metres, when it suddenly slammed on brakes and was engulfed in a cloud of dust. As the dust parted, I could make out what looked like Asian tourists, each one of them with a camera of some sort in hand, madly taking pictures of something. I looked back towards the film set and there loping between the thick bush and thorn trees was the enormous head and neck of a Tyrannosaurus Rex, making its way down the hill. The camera crew were invisible, out of sight behind a thicket. You can only imagine the shock, terror and utter disbelief experienced by that hapless group of tourists. Needless to say, the tour-bus didn't stay long. It reversed swiftly, backing up into the bushes, did a U-turn and left. I have never laughed so hard in my life!

To this day, somewhere in deepest Asia there is a family or two who went home after their safari believing that somewhere in the African bush a Tyrannosaurus Rex roams free!

A few years later, the production was released on television and there, walking through the Umfolozi Game Reserve, was the Tyrannosaurus Rex doing his thing. I laughed, knowing that somewhere, way to the right of the shot, were some horribly confused tourists.

....

CHAPTER 22

MANDELA'S HELICOPTER

Accentuate the positive and eliminate the negative.

'm always interested when I hear people commenting on Nelson Mandela. Even though years have passed since he left us on the 5th of December 2013, I am still attentive to anyone who comes up to me to share a story or an encounter they had with this astonishing man.

The stories I hear are fascinating insights into not only Mandela's character, but how people related to him. Very often, I use this to calibrate my own interactions with him, through this understanding of how the world outside of Mandela's immediate circle perceived and understood him to be.

I was out to lunch one day with a few people, when a woman, who had been listening to our conversation about Mandela, leant over from her table and proceeded to tell me why she didn't like him. Usually, I'd tell the person to mind their own business, but I was intrigued by her rather blunt remark.

"Anyone who smiles that much shouldn't be trusted."

The group I was with all muttered to themselves, in response to her statement. Finally, they all turned to me to ask my thoughts on what she had said. I laughed and said that she was correct, Mandela had indeed smiled a lot, then dropping my voice and becoming more sombre, I said,

"Thank heavens he was constantly smiling! He devoted his entire life to reaching out, building bridges, empowering others, so that people like you could be liberated and have even a glimmer of hope for a brighter future."

I don't think I have ever expressed myself with such conviction. It crystallised what I had always thought and believed, but I had not verbally expressed it until that point.

I didn't stop there.

"Ma'am, Mandela used education to not only transform himself, but the lives of countless others. I'm not sure if you know this, but whilst in prison, he instructed all the other prisoners on Robben Island to use their time to educate themselves. At one point, they used to joke that it was no longer the Robben Island Prison, but the University of Robben Island. He told his fellow prisoners that when they were eventually free, they would need to lead this nation."

The group that had now gathered didn't say a word, so I continued.

"Mandela had three prison warders throughout his prison years: Christo Brand, James Gregory and Jack Swart. Mandela saw to it that the children of these warders were educated right the way through to university level. Why do you think he did that? Would you educate your enemy? He did this to end the indoctrination and ignorance of the past, to break the cycle that is passed on from one generation to the next. I'll be the first to admit that Mandela was no saint and that he had many flaws, but to write him off because he chose to smile does not show a lack of trustworthiness on Mandela's part, but sadly it reflects your own ignorance and lack of understanding of what he aspired to in leading this country."

The woman shrugged her shoulders, let out a surprised, almost inaudible sound and left.

The years that I had spent in the presence of Mandela allowed far more than mere photographic opportunities. They gave me an opportunity to observe who this man really was. I spent many hours researching as much as I could about his life. I wasn't trying to find flaws in his character; I was merely trying to gain a better understanding of who he was. I will admit that he was far from saintly. However, if there are tiers below sainthood, I would place Nelson Mandela on the next rung down.

I observed a man who had truly journeyed in his life. He was at such ease with the world because he had transcended so much of what we all battle to overcome, day in and day out. My biggest revelation was that Mandela's selfless sacrifice of his own freedom in the fight to end apartheid and to liberate all the people of South Africa was not the cause of his greatest pain and suffering. For Mandela, 'the struggle' and imprisonment brought about an isolation and separation from those he loved, his wife and children. Therein lay his greatest pain and suffering. In my opinion, I felt he had abandoned them.

Mandela's imprisonment was so inhumane that some will be offended with any argument that it had a positive effect on him. The truth is aspects of prison did benefit Mandela. The relative isolation over all those years narrowed his focus. He was able to isolate his thoughts and hone in on what was most relevant with remarkable detail and revelation, without all the distractions of modern life. He did not need to earn money; he had no place to be or meetings to attend. He was in prison. He followed prison rules. Time was all he had, and he used that time to consider deeply the things that he and his fellow inmates discussed and grappled with. It is documented that, in later years, Mandela often longed for that silence and peace he had found in prison. He used his time wisely. He harnessed the positive aspects of a very dire and seemingly hopeless situation.

If there is a third insight that I can add at this point, it is this. I believe that Mandela, like so many other long-term prisoners, did indeed have elements of institutionalised behaviour. The one thing the apartheid government never broke was his mind. In that aspect, Mandela won hands down. I do not believe that he suffered from institutionalised behaviour in that regard. It was evidenced more in the practical way that Mandela undertook certain tasks. It is well documented that Mandela was very particular and followed a strict regimen. Much of it, I imagine, stemmed from living in a confined space with set rules and regulations.

Mandela, I believe, could have freed himself at many points during his 27 years in prison. He could have turned his back on the armed struggle and returned to his rural homeland, leaving the white government to continue their agenda. The conditions of his proposed release were clear. His determination to remain in prison and gain freedom for all meant that he had to shoulder the burden of not being there for his family. Mandela may not have expressed this openly, but I could sense it when he was with his family. I believe that he carried it in his heart all the remaining days of his life.

By the time I came to work with him, I was witnessing the life of a man, sober in his actions and words, who knew and understood the complexity and costs of the sacrifice that he had made for his people. He had travelled to the very edge of human suffering, and in so doing liberated not only himself but an entire nation.

I have always appreciated how much Madiba loved his rural homelands. Many times in his book, *The Long Walk to Freedom*, Mandela referred to his childhood and to his love for the rolling hills around Qunu and Mvezo. It was as if this special affection was the one thing that the apartheid government could not take away from him.

If I remember correctly, it was a year before the soccer World Cup in 2010. It was midsummer, and I found myself out in the rural areas of Mvezo, a place I had been many times before. This time was a little different. I had joined a group of press journalists and photographers awaiting the arrival of Nelson Mandela by helicopter. We were gathered on top of the hill overlooking the Mbhashe River. It was a stinking hot day; the sun was out in full force and, with no shade or a breath of wind anywhere, people's tempers were frayed.

Coming in from the north, as if by stealth, flying low over the undulating hills, I caught sight of a South African Airforce Oryx helicopter. Within seconds of my spotting it, we were all watching it make a low flypast, bank hard to the left and then circle the entire Mvezo homestead, following the course of the river. The helicopter levelled off then made another wide angle turn, this time to the right, reversing its route back up along the arc of the river, flying back over us to the landing pad not far away.

I was excited beyond words. I love any flying machine, especially when it is hovering overhead, so this was enough to blow my mind. The helicopter had passed over us so low that I could smell the fumes from its exhaust. The rotor blades thumped the air hard as it banked before hovering and coming down to earth in an almighty cloud of dust. This beast of a machine had made its entrance in dramatic fashion and rightly so. It was carrying within it our most cherished asset.

My enjoyment of the occasion and all the anticipation and drama of this arrival was rudely interrupted by the vapid utterings of a British journalist mouthing off in foul language about how the pilot was causing us all such headaches by repeatedly blasting us with the helicopter's noise. Why couldn't he simply arrive and land? I swung around and uncharacteristically told the man to

"Shut the fuck up!"

Mandela, when occasions allowed, asked the pilot if he could be treated to flying over the place of his birth before coming in to land. This small request gave Madiba the opportunity to get the best views of the place he loved and cherished so much.

The journalist stood there blinking at me. I hadn't meant for it to come out so forcefully, but I had lost patience with these international journalists who are so cock-sure of themselves, marching around my country, fingering everything with their disapproval and negativity. You could never talk to one of them without them going off about all the countries and war-torn locations they had reported on and put themselves through. It was as if they carried their sufferings around like badges pinned to their chests. They had so little respect for who we were, what our cultures meant to us and the reverence we gave to those who had sacrificed their lives so that we could continue to fulfil our highest ideals as a nation. It always infuriated me. A few of the South African journalists rallied around me and gave a collective grunt before turning their backs on this now isolated individual.

There was a negative aspect to the hype around Mandela. Often you'd hear his bodyguards saying in frustration,

"Enough pictures! How many do you have to take? It's enough!"

Whenever Mandela moved about in public, he was followed by a pack of journalists. I had often observed this, but seldom experienced it from 'inside the throng'. I was caught up in this mob by mistake one day. I ended up on my knees, pushed to one side by the pack. I wasn't the only one on the floor. The bubbly, well-respected South African photographer, Alf Khumalo had also been shoved to the ground. He was a man in his seventies and this made me mad. Using my own weight and height, I pushed my back into the mass of people, creating the space Alf needed to get back up. Whilst making sure that he had all his equipment, I looked past him and there was Madiba sitting watching intently. He had witnessed the whole scene and now looked on with deep concern. Madiba had known Alf Khumalo for many years and had obviously recognised him in the crowd. Once he had established that we were both okay, Madiba nodded and went back to what he was doing.

....

A HARSH REALITY AND THE MADE-UP DREAM!

"Faith is a risk, but it is one that I would not want to live without."
- Desmond Tutu

Perched above Sunset Boulevard in West Hollywood, the Chateau Marmont hotel is an impressive 1920s French-styled, castle-like building. The who's who of Hollywood and the silver screen have come here over the years to be seen, party up a storm, or to do business as they sign record contracts and movie deals. Its history is as old as Hollywood itself.

While driving through from Santa Monica, I received a call letting me know that friends had managed to get a table at the Chateau that evening, and asking if I'd like to join them. If you want to dine anywhere notable in LA, you don't set foot out of the door unless you have booked way in advance. The night before, we'd eaten at 'The Ivy' along Robertson Boulevard with some executives from HBO television. Our table of five had been booked a few months before! It was fascinating soaking up what it was like to live, work and play in Los Angeles. It's a fascinating world that is so surreal that it's sometimes like being on a real-life movie set.

I had no idea of the history of the place when I entered the Chateau that evening. You could feel the buzz as our group arrived on the main floor. In front of us was a large lounge with heavy, draped curtains. Larger than life sofas filled the room. In addition, there were side lamps, coffee tables and a beautiful grand piano tucked away to the right as we came down a few stairs into the lounge. The patio restaurant was packed. The atmosphere was fantastic, people laughed and talked enthusiastically. A few people gave us the once over as we made our way to our table. This was the place to be seen, where the famous let their hair down, Hollywood-style.

Much later in the evening, we adjourned to the lounge, found a spot on the sofas and continued to enjoy the wonderful atmosphere. It was late summer; the air was warm and I felt alive, privileged to be meeting and talking to new and exciting people so far from home.

As the drinks kept coming, our bravery increased and by midnight we were all gathered around the piano, singing away to whatever the pianist was playing. If I knew the name of the young pianist, I would sing his praises. He was a human jukebox. Whatever was requested, he knew and we all sang along in chorus.

At the stroke of midnight, the pianist stood up and bid us farewell. He had another gig across town. We applauded his sheer talent, and all grumbled that our jukebox was no more. With nothing to lose and brave beyond sobriety, I simply sat down at the piano and asked what song was next. I certainly was nowhere near as good and I knew only a handful of songs, but play I did. The party was on again, and in no time, gathered around the piano were a Russian oligarch with his two blond models, a Texan, two rich looking Eastern European ladies and some locals, who all did a fabulous job of singing long after midnight.

With a flight to catch to New York at 10am the next morning, I knew it was time to leave. We pulled ourselves away from the lounge, bowed to everyone still enjoying the evening and headed for our waiting cars. As we made our way through the reception area, a smartly dressed gentleman came up to me, asking if he could have a word. I recognised him from earlier in the evening. He introduced himself as the manager that evening at the Chateau. Either I was in trouble or had left something behind. I apologised profusely for disrespecting the ambiance of the lounge and his patrons. I told him he would never see me again as I was from South Africa and would probably never return to his hotel. The words literally fell out my mouth as I tried to pre-empt any possible argument.

Surprisingly, he held out his hand for me to shake and laughed.

"No, sir, I wanted to say thank you. We haven't seen that spirit here for a long time at the Chateau. If this is your last time here, then let me leave you with a gift. This is an old hotel and if the walls could talk, I am sure they'd include you in their stories. But I want you to remember this; the piano you have just played has been there for over 60 years. You have joined an impressive list of entertainers who, as you did this evening, just sat down and started to play. The keys of that piano have been played by some of the greatest entertainers the world has ever seen: Frank Sinatra, Elvis Presley, Nina Simone, Elton John, Liza Minnelli, have all sat at that piano … take that back to Africa with you."

We all stood there, looking up at the ceiling, trying to absorb his words in the final moments of my time at the Chateau.

"Ah, sir, thank you for saying that. You see, long ago where I live on the east coast of Southern Africa, I was told that I'd never be a Hollywood star and that my dream was unrealistic. But if what you say is true, then even if only for a few moments in my life, I got to entertain here in Hollywood. The curse has been broken and I did make it in Hollywood!"

We all laughed, and handshakes soon turned into great big bear hugs. Our elevator arrived. We climbed in and said goodbye to Hollywood.

In fact, that whole day had been a bit surreal. Before the Chateau, I'd spent the long afternoon looking out over the Pacific Ocean lost in my own world, walking up and down Santa Monica beach. Earlier that day, I had been with a good friend on set in downtown Los Angeles, watching the making of Maroon 5's latest music video, entitled *Animals*. I had never been on a music video set before, and was fascinated by how it all worked and of course, watching a real rock band go through the motions of recording a music video.

The producer had invited us into his trailer to relax. They were all waiting for the lead singer of the band, Adam Levine, to arrive for his recording. It was lunch time. LA was stinking hot, so it was pleasant to relax in the plush trailer. The producer's kids played around inside, oblivious to this world their parents were creating, this industry of music, video and fame.

Soon the engine of a Harley Davidson was heard outside. The producer jumped up and swung the door of the trailer open and the mood immediately changed. Adam Levine had arrived. I peered out through the door and caught a glimpse of the two of them laughing and joking together; they obviously knew each other. Even though the mood was relaxed, I had a sense that time was money and all the various personalities had to be managed.

We had been there all morning and had to be on our way. I had hoped to meet Adam, but it was not to be.

On our way out, I had hoped to catch a glimpse of Adam so I drove past the trailers very slowly. The door of one of the trailers swung open and Adam Levine stepped out. He had a group of people fussing over him, from hairstylists to make up artists, even a few people with headphones talking to whoever was back in the warehouse where they were filming. This was my chance. I stopped the car, climbed out and walked right over to him. I was leaving anyway, so it wouldn't matter if security kicked up a fuss. I joined the crowd walking at pace towards the warehouse film set. We shook hands. I said I was leaving, but that it was good to meet him. He gave me a high five and said that he'd love to chat, but he was already late and the producer was screaming at everyone in his earpiece. I laughed. Of course he was. I turned and made my way back to my car with engine still running. Just then I heard someone calling. I swung around not sure if I'd done something wrong, but there, halfway between me and the warehouse, Adam Levine had turned and was calling out to me.

"Hey, you're the one from South Africa? Mandela, right?"

"Yes, sir!" I called back.

"Was good to meet you. I love Mandela; thanks for coming!" He gave me a thumbs up, and just like that, he turned back into his own world and was gone.

My only guess was that one of the assistant producers in the group around him had told him that I was visiting from South Africa and had worked with Mandela.

Many times, I've had similar fleeting moments of interaction that could never have been planned. At the Vienna State Ballet, I shared a canteen dinner with the opera singer, Placido Domingo.

He happened to be doing a show at the Opera whilst I was photographing the ballet. One of the most surreal opportunities I have ever experienced was standing at the podium of the United Nations Assembly in New York City; the same podium where the most loved and equally most reviled leaders of nations for the past 60 years had stood to address the world.

I've looked out at audiences from stages only a precious few get to perform on, from the Royal Opera stage in Covent Garden, London, to the Vienna State Opera stage in Austria. I've allowed presidents to reflect on their pasts, drawn words out of leaders in business, and waited in line to shake the hands of men and women that have changed the world. When I was 10 years old, I sat on the shoulders of a German missionary nun in a large crowd, just to catch a glimpse of Mother Theresa on her first visit to South Africa. Her Missionaries of Charity were one of the first organisations to make a home in South Africa just before the fall of apartheid. Later that day I met her, with a group of other children who made a path for her leading from the church to her waiting car.

In the spring of 2017, I stood in front of 300 people gathered in the halls of the National Underground Railroad Freedom Center in Cincinnati, Ohio. I had been invited to officially open one of the most intimate and definitive museum exhibitions created in the United States on the life and legacy of Nelson Mandela. The exhibition consisted predominantly of my own work, and was the result of a labour of love over the previous four years. The audience I stood before was as foreign and diverse as I could ever have imagined. That opening marked the zenith of my entire life's work to date, the culmination of a journey that began with the simple dream to one day shake the hand of Nelson Mandela. You'd think I would have scripted the perfect speech weeks in advance, but with so much going on, I found myself awake at 4am, sitting in my hotel room some 23 storeys up, frantically writing the speech. How do you distil twenty years of work and endeavour into twenty minutes?

There was no way, as a sixteen-year-old boy standing in the streets of Durban, watching Mandela make a speech, that I could have known it was the beginning of a journey that would culminate in the privilege of sharing the life of Nelson Mandela with the people of America. I have never settled for 'the next best thing'. I crave experiences that extend my boundaries. I find myself constantly resetting the horizons of my view on life, striving to expand the group of people I have met and analysing the lessons that life has taught me.

However, constantly stepping out and finding yourself in new places, interacting with new people, can also be a humbling leveller when things go wrong.

At the start of each new venture, I have found myself needing to step out into the void and then work at keeping the ball rolling, often independently. I have also learnt not to sign my life away in contracts. During the early years of running my own business, I made many mistakes and I began to believe that people were conniving and would do their utmost to own me or to have me beholden to them. I didn't start out cynical but often whilst out there making things happen, shaking hands, smiling and delivering on my own creativity, I found myself battling the darker side of the photographic world.

Success is never achieved without difficulties and consequences, that's for sure. While in school, I discovered photography. I began to share the results of my activities, one of which was a photo taken from the top of an extremely tall Norfolk Pine tree within the school grounds. I had scaled this goliath of a tree one afternoon after school. Unfortunately, a few teachers noticed. This act had repercussions. I was happy to accept the punishment meted out because whilst up there, clinging to the spindly branches in a stiff breeze, I had taken a photo looking out over the whole school. In the ensuing years, both the story and the image have become part of the school's folklore, not so much as a result of the image but because whilst up there, I had tied a pair of underpants to the top branches; for many years, they served as a cheeky symbol of my defiance. I was punished for scaling the tree, and the school couldn't very well ask me to remove them without placing me in more danger. There was no way, save chopping down the tree that they could be removed. So, there they stayed for many years. I had never intended for my odd 'flag' perched on top of the tree, to be any form of defiance. It was supposed to be a confirmation of something I had achieved, an indication that I was prepared to risk temporary pain in order to see a new horizon.

Many years later, I had saved what I could and spent two weeks photographing New York City, creating some fantastic images. Soon after returning back home, I opened an exhibition of my work from New York City. Those who attended the opening were unaware that I had misunderstood how international roaming worked on mobile phones. I discovered that upon my return, I had racked up a bill of R42 000. Roaming, it turned out was a killer, with exorbitant costs per megabyte used. I had been oblivious to this. So instead of making a profit on my images, I was selling them off in order to pay my hefty cell phone bill.

Perhaps my hardest lesson whilst trying to push my career to new heights came in the form of a well-dressed, ostentatious woman who appeared at an exhibition I was doing in Germany. She swept me up in her tentacles of lies and deceit with promises of riches and fame. She claimed to know individuals of high net worth in Europe. Her promises were the oil to my desire to be successful in Europe. I was convinced that my time had come and that this woman was my ticket to fast-tracking up the ladder of success. I never once stopped to question why I needed an agent as I had been pretty successful on my own.

I should have taken note of the alarm bells when she expressed an urgency to sign a contract before I left for the airport the next day. In hindsight, I should have known that contracts take time to compile and negotiate and should be read over by a lawyer before signing. I should have done my research into what an artist /agent contractual agreement looked like. Essentially, I had the ability and I should have respected my value as an artist. But I didn't, and it led to three years of utter pain and anguish. When people hurt me, I'm generally able to work my way through it, and in time I'm able to forgive them and move on with life. That cannot be said in this instance. Only when it was too late, did I realize what I had signed. The contract was equivalent to signing my own death warrant as an artist. I have never in my life had to fight so hard for my own independence and rights as an artist. I experienced first-hand levels of deceit, bitterness and evil I hope never to encounter again. I lost hundreds of thousands of rand over those three years. It affected me both emotionally and financially. It left me physically ill for an extended period of time and took years to get over. I became disillusioned with others and cut myself off from friends. Worst of all, I was unable to be creative. I descended into a tormented and isolated world from which it took a number of years to recover.

It's easy to look back now and pinpoint where I went wrong. I wanted the easy way out. I can say it now; I had been tempted by greed and laziness, seeing the opportunity to make money through an agent who I thought would bring me wealth. She would do all the work and I would just arrive, shake hands, sign books and enjoy the fun part. Fortunately, with the help of friends in Europe and South Africa, I was able to retrieve all my photographic artworks and terminate the contract, which for a while had threatened to destroy me. I understand it now and it's something I can now advise other artists on. It has only been through my own acceptance of where I went wrong, that I have been able to forgive and to move on.

As artists we are vulnerable in the business world; we don't understand or appreciate the binding terms of contracts and at times we don't think rationally. We hunger for recognition and remuneration and gravitate to those who promise to make us successful overnight. I like to go about my work believing in people's integrity to behave in a manner that is honouring and carries a certain element of goodwill. Sadly, not all agents and sponsors behave as we expect. We need to become wise and vigilant, both personally and in defence of others.

Survival comes in many forms. If there is survival on the business front, then survival out in the field of operation is a whole new ballgame. Few appreciate what one has to endure in order to capture some brilliant images whilst on assignment, documenting in far-flung places.

I made the fatal mistake on a trip with the NGO, Oxfam Australia, working out in rural Northern KwaZulu-Natal, of not going to the toilet first thing in the morning. By 10am after a three-hour drive, we were in the thick of the African bush, working with rural herders and their cattle. I sensed that I had at most about two minutes to find a place to go to the toilet. There wasn't a large rock or tree anywhere in sight, so I excused myself from a few very confused herdsmen, and walked right into the centre of perhaps 100 head of cattle, pulled down my pants and with great relief sorted my problem out. I sat there perched on a tiny rock committed to my ablutions, completely surrounded by the hindquarters of rural cattle with their swooshing tails flicking away thousands of flies.

A few years previously, I was out in South/Central Mozambique working for an aid agency backed by the United Nations. Our group had pitched camp on the outskirts of a village. It was one of many that had initially been decimated by severe flooding and then almost immediately hit with five years of severe drought. We arrived towards the end of the drought and witnessed communities who, without food aid, would simply vanish. Day after day we worked to build sustainable projects through food and water security practices. I watched as people stood in long lines stretching for kilometres, just to receive a meagre ration of rice, a few packets of beans and cooking oil. I have no idea if anything we introduced in that period has been sustained or worked long-term. I know that we did succeed in addressing the immediate need to feed people and to stave off the famine.

Our group of seven people had committed two weeks to going where the need was greatest. Leaving Maputo, we typed in some global positioning points and headed north-east, following roads, bush paths and train tracks to get us out into the middle of where things had gone horribly wrong. It took us three long, hard days to arrive at our destination. We met with the local chiefs who helped bring us up to speed on developments, then set up camp and started to work. It wasn't as if we worked out in the field and then returned to luxury accommodation. Our accommodation was just as rustic as that of the villagers around us. We lined our beds up under a large marula tree, dug a pit latrine in the bushes, and made the fire-place the central gathering spot of our open, sandy spot with a couple of chairs.

The locals generally left us alone. Every now and then, small kids would come and visit but generally there was no entertainment in the evenings. Often, we sat around the fire talking about the day's work, how to improve the next day's work or discussed our schedule.

The days were hot and humid and the evenings cool. At night, lying in my sleeping bag, I welcomed the rest and time alone with my thoughts. We all looked forward to this time of day, not only because it allowed us to be alone with our thoughts, but because of the miracle of what was happening above us each night. As we looked up through the branches of the marula tree, there, stretching from one horizon to the other was a universe of unimaginable stars. On the horizon, peeks of light from the fires in front of straw huts surrounded us, but looking up, we witnessed a vision that defied any description. We fell asleep aware of the incredibly rare privilege of being out here doing this work.

But if the nights of dropping off to sleep were quiet, meditative and peaceful, the mornings were quite the opposite. I've slept through some unnerving noises on my adventures, but nothing had prepared me for this.

It began each day at around 3am, when we should have been enjoying our deepest sleep, knowing that another 15-hour day awaited us. In the distance, sounded the squawk of a single rooster – one of those scraggly fowls that we'd seen scratching around in the dirt between the huts. Silence descended ... until, on the other side of the village, a second rooster, not to be outdone by the first, would crow at the top of his lungs. The second bird hauled us out of our deep sleep. Irritated, I'd roll over and stuff the pillow over my head in an attempt to sleep. However, I only had a few seconds of respite before it all began. At first, two or three roosters would crow, but as each confirmed its position, the chorus grew. Within a few minutes, a dozen roosters would become hundreds of roosters, a cacophony of noise rising from wherever each had made his roost the evening before. You have never in your life heard such a noise. It was so loud, I felt as if I had made my bed in the middle of Times Square, New York City. I have never felt so nauseous and delirious. I felt completely helpless; there was nothing I could do to shut them up. The noise lasted for close to an hour before everything went quiet again. Overcome with shock and feeling severely defeated, I sank back into deep sleep, but only for another hour at most. Sleeping outdoors on the flatlands of Mozambique, there is nothing to protect you from the fireball that blasts its light sideways into your retina the second it appears above the horizon. The sun became the new enemy.

Mornings were the hardest. We wore shoes wherever we went; there was no telling what worms or other parasites lived on the sandy ground. We made sure to wash our hands and faces as often as possible. All other cleaning was secondary. Toilet detail was dreaded most of all. The only thicket of bush that offered any sort of privacy was along the pathway that the villagers used to go about their daily business. The best we could hope for was to have a bowel movement early in the morning when other people weren't around. When we did go, we made sure to face our bum-cheeks towards the path so that we could hide our faces. That way, anyone who did come along wouldn't recognise us immediately. One of our Italian team-members overlooked this necessity and had to endure a long conversation with a villager who recognised him – all whilst relieving himself, squatting over a hole in the ground. Naturally, things became far more complicated if we developed diarrhoea. Sadly, I experienced this first-hand. At that point, even if the entire village comes to chat to you, dignity and privacy are the last things on your mind.

Living such a rustic lifestyle while trying to keep your camera equipment dust free, is hard work. The first two days are somewhat of an adventure: things are new, you have energy and you're keen to get out there. The days after that become an endurance race; things become an effort and you start to miss urban comforts. Mood swings occur quickly and you have to keep a constant check on yourself.

During the last two days, you begin to anticipate leaving. With the thought of being able to leave, your energy returns and your mood changes. On my last evening in Mozambique, I took a walk along the vast network of paths that crisscrossed the village. Not far from our camp, I discovered a young baobab tree growing. From the look of it, I could tell that it had the space to become, over the next few hundred years, an almighty tree whose branches would reach out over the bushlands, with views for hundreds of miles around. Already, at its relatively young age, I got the sense that this tree was strong, free of injury or disease. For some reason, this baobab gave me hope; its presence motivated me to believe in the bigger picture of life.

I won't lie; I hated that place. Although I was grateful for the unique experience and the opportunity to capture some thought-provoking images, despite this, I felt the need to leave behind something that recorded that point in my life and the things I had dealt with during the past two weeks. So, I found a sharp stone, selected a spot on the trunk of the tree that faced the setting sun and carved two letters into the fleshy, fibrous skin of the tree. To this day, I have no idea where exactly in that part of country I was. I have no idea the name of the village or the name of the chief, but somewhere on the plains of Mozambique, a baobab tree grows with two letters that face the setting African sun each evening engraved on its trunk. I will never see that tree again, but its memory will be with me for the rest of my life.

Never once during my studies did I ever think that I would make this type of photography a part of my life. I wanted to be in advertising or fashion. Surely my years of dance would give me a keen eye. The privilege to photograph for aid agencies and organisations came to me. I certainly never went looking for it. My goal was to work at the level of high art, yet my career path had cemented itself around issues and problems within communities on the periphery of life. From day one, I admit that I struggled with the challenges of meeting humanity at the coal face of life. I embraced the experience because I loved the adventure it offered me. I felt I needed it to toughen me up, to show others what I was capable of enduring and creating. In a warped way, my going out to photograph HIV/AIDS, tuberculosis, malaria, drought and disease were all badges that I pinned on myself. I strutted around, thinking I was better than others because I was out there doing my bit for humanity while they weren't.

It wasn't until I turned 30 that the wheels started to come off. I developed an inability to form close relationships with people. I pushed people away and abhorred any physical contact. I would wash my hands and face over and over. I became petrified that I had become one with those people I had watched dying, or worse, that I was infected with their diseases. No amount of rationalising could convince me otherwise. I had gained a vast knowledge of my subject matter, but instead of edifying me, it had crawled under my skin and was destroying me from the inside out.

Death never leaves you. It sits on you. If left unresolved, it can begin to eat away at your life. Many of us have seen poverty. Those living in Africa are very familiar with it. We are continually exposed to the needs that exist, and we observe daily how conditions deteriorate. Yet few of us actually step out from behind our walls of fear to actively engage with the issues that poverty encompasses.

I certainly didn't until a good friend of mine and one of the Senior Directors of Oxfam International in Melbourne, Australia, noticed something was wrong. Whilst chatting with me, he noticed things weren't quite right. I was booked off work, and appointments were made for me to see a psychologist. Through counselling, everything was exposed. The consequence of years and years of feeling as impenetrable as a young man marching off to war armed with my camera, thinking that I was strong and that nothing could penetrate my armour, finally surfaced. It took a further two years of working through it all before I felt strong enough to sign myself up again for shoots with a few aid agencies in Southern Africa. I didn't touch HIV and AIDS or any disease-related topics. Instead, I chose to work on water and sanitation health-care issues in rural and semi-formal settlements in and around the area where I lived.

One of these assignments took me to rural Ixopo. The first few days I was fine. I was creating again; it felt good to be back in the saddle. On the fourth day, it all fell apart. We were working deep in the rural districts surrounding Ixopo. The focus of my assignment was to investigate government-built pit latrines. Essentially, they were large pits dug in the ground, covered by a concrete block with an open hole. When the pit was full of human waste, they simply dug a new hole and moved the concrete block to the new pit.

I was coping well until I learnt how toddlers were falling into these holes and drowning in human waste. It was as if a switch had been flipped in my brain. I literally fell apart. I lost control of the situation. I became emotional; I began to lash out at people, blaming everyone I saw for what was going on. My objectivity as a professional had been compromised. With 15 years of experience, having never once let my clients down, I made the call. I made the decision to remove myself and cancelled the commission. I climbed into my car and left. I had spent 15 years striving to make a difference, working across Southern and Eastern Africa from Ethiopia to Lesotho, and in the end, I lost.

Many photographers have published books dealing with wars and the depraved human conditions that exist in those environments. Many discuss the horrors of what they encountered whilst documenting, and how the conditions broke them in the end. Some became alcoholics; others took to drugs or suffered broken relationships. Some, like me, just shrivelled up inside, with more questions than answers.

For my part, I managed to find a partial solution. I have chosen to channel my energies into accentuating the positive. Although I still photograph some of the subjects discussed above, I'm careful to acknowledge my sensitivities and vulnerabilities. I am no longer the hero riding into battle, thinking my images will save lives. That's ego. I am saving no one. At most, I am highlighting through dramatic and powerful images, what we've become and need to address.

I remember a few years back, sitting in a lounge talking with Archbishop Desmond Tutu one morning. The conversation wasn't at all deep, but in his matter of fact way, the Arch moved onto the topic of faith. He said that faith was a risk, but that it was a risk he was willing to take. I've always had faith. As a boy, I'd be in constant conversation with Jesus through-out the highs and lows. That faith and conversation continues to this day.

....

CHAPTER 24

FAME, FORTUNE AND BEAUTIFUL WOMEN

I used to think special moments just happen, until I discovered how hard it was to shake Nelson Mandela's hand.

A few days after I had my unfortunate run in with the President of Mexico, I attended a dinner party hosted by the former Prime Minister of Ireland, Mary Robinson. It was a lavish event, held in the ballroom of Dublin Castle.

We have all, at some point in our lives, stood in long queues at some famous building to purchase an entrance ticket. Like little flocks of sheep, we have moved down passages peering into hallowed places, careful not to touch anything. I've certainly done it countless times. So it was surreal to find myself chauffeur-driven from my hotel to Dublin Castle and to be greeted there by the first woman Prime Minister of Ireland. With a small group of fellow guests, I entered the castle; we were taken up the grand staircase for a social meet and greet, before being ushered through to our seats in the adjoining ballroom, at the longest dinner table I had seen in my life.

The atmosphere was very relaxed. I was one of the last to arrive. By the time I was handed a glass of champagne and a bite to eat from a silver tray that miraculously appeared before me, everyone attending was in good spirits, laughing and enjoying the evening.

Not knowing many people – not personally knowing anyone that is, but certainly recognising almost everyone – I took a deep breath and wandered into the room. With all the airs and graces I could muster, I smiled and shook hands. I wandered into conversations, only to hear them talk about summer holidays in the south of France or an evening they'd shared with so and so.

Of course, none of them knew who I was and, as often happens at a gathering of this nature, when you don't know someone you treat them with utmost respect, whilst asking polite questions in an attempt to guess their identity. This became our mutual goal.

A waiter came around to a group I thought interesting enough to join, so I used the opportunity of choosing something off the silverware to join the group. I found myself talking to a group of British guests. Everyone in the group was about my height, except for one lady, whose head was well below our shoulders. I recognised her immediately as Dame Ellen MacArthur, the first female yachtswoman to single-handedly circumnavigate the globe. I wasn't too sure who the others were, but they were all having an intense conversation about the planet and the impact we as humans were having on it. I was keen to get in on the conversation, so I introduced myself and made sure to mention my work in development across southern and eastern Africa. Fortunately, this struck a chord with the group, and I began to field a barrage of questions about Africa, its leadership, my thoughts about illicit diamond mining and the slave labour which was rife in Africa. Not that I had any meaningful answer to any of those questions. Typically, I had thrown myself in the deep end and was now required to swim. The last thing I needed was another Mexican President situation, so I quipped that I lived somewhere deep in Africa, far from civilisation, and politely asked who I was speaking to.

They all laughed and one by one they introduced themselves. I joked that I knew who Ellen was, then panicked a bit when the world-famous photographer, Yann Arthus-Betrand, shook my hand. I was totally confused when the last man, a well-dressed, black gentleman, introduced himself as Michael Hastings. One of the people in the group corrected him, and reintroduced him as Lord Michael Hastings. I responded with respect and continued to play on my ignorance of European etiquette. I was intrigued. He took a keen interest in my work with Nelson Mandela and I fielded some pretty heavy questions about Mandela's leadership.

As we chatted, I grew more and more fascinated as to who Lord Hastings was. The only time I had ever come across the name Hastings was at school, when we'd learnt about the Battle of Hastings in 1066. He was certainly a fascinating man. If I had known more about his career and appointments, I'd probably not have been so bold in entering the group to join their conversation. I later learnt that Lord Hastings' career portfolio included Vice-Presidency of UNICEF, KPMG's International Global Head of Corporate Citizenship, an appointment to the House of Lords by HRH Queen Elizabeth II and being the BBC's first Head of Corporate Social Responsibility. What surprised me more was how relaxed he was and how willing he was to openly engage with me and ask so many questions. We became so engrossed in our conversation that Dame MacArthur, Yann Arthus-Betrand and the others moved off. I had finally made a friend from this galaxy of leaders in their respective fields.

Keen to meet others in the room, we parted ways and it wasn't long before I spotted someone I considered the most interesting sports personality in the room, the former tennis star, Boris Becker.

Fortunately, he was standing alone, trying to politely eat one of the hors d'oeuvres, which gave me an opening to politely introduce myself. Cutting to the chase, I used the opportunity to ask a question that had plagued me for years.

"Is Roger Federer all that? In the opinion of a man in your position, with your insight into the game and the whole industry, is he really that good?"

"That's such a big question. Why are you asking me that?"

"I've never met the man and I have only ever watched his career on television. You are the first person within the ATP Tour I've met and had the opportunity to ask."

"You do know I'm the coach of his opposition, Novak Djokovic, right?"

"Yes, that's why I know that whatever you say will have huge meaning."

"I tell you what, there are too many people around, let's enjoy our evening, and you come find me after and I'll tell you."

With that he turned and walked away, leaving me a bit let down, but even more keen to hear what he had to say. I think he was hoping I'd forget and he'd dodge having to answer the question.

The tall doors to the ballroom opened and we all filed in. Ushers showed us to our places at the extraordinarily long dinner table. It was astonishing to find myself seated at a table that ran down the centre of the ballroom, surrounded by immaculate decorations and architecture dating back hundreds of years. The play of light on the royal blue carpet, the pronounced pillars and walls shaded in the same royal blue lined with gold paint, was breath-taking. Adding to the grandeur of the place, I felt a sense of its medieval history. High up near the ceiling, running the length of the ballroom, were flags which I could only guess represented the different counties or clans of the Irish nation.

I found myself seated with a beautiful woman on my left and keeping me in my place, seated on my right, the world-renowned photographer, Yann Arthus-Betrand. His English wasn't that good, which was a pity, as I'd willingly have spent the whole evening asking questions and listening to him speak. Instead, I enjoyed the whole evening laughing and talking to easily the best-looking woman at the table. I remember, upon standing up after dinner, how Yann Arthus-Betrand joked that he never wanted to sit next to me again, because he wasn't able to get a word in with the beautiful woman I was sitting next to. We all laughed, but coming from a Frenchman who no doubt loved the attention of women, there was some truth behind his words.

I was sad to leave the castle with all its grandeur. It was the first time I'd actually been in such a building and seen it used for its intended purpose, rather than as a museum or relic of its country's past. The rain had started to fall, so a few of us piled into a waiting chauffeur-driven Mercedes Benz. We returned to our hotel, intent on carrying on what was proving to be an exciting evening.

The hotel lobby was buzzing with guests, all waiting to mingle with the more famous personalities staying at the hotel. I happened to get talking to Richard Branson's son, Sam Branson. I had met his father in South Africa a few years back and remembered he had a game lodge called Ulusaba, near the Kruger National Park. It grabbed Sam's attention and he was genuinely surprised I knew of it. I was just glad that I had remembered, as it made for easy conversation with him. Unlike me, he knew many of the people present that evening. It was all too easy to stand there and by default have people eager to shake my hand through association with Sam Branson. At one point, we were joined by a Mr Michiel Mol. Immediately, the conversation changed and for some reason they started talking about spaceships and rockets. It turned out that Michiel Mol was the founding member of XCOR Space Expeditions, a space exploration company in direct competition with Sam's father in the race to getting tourists into orbit. Here were two men obviously in the super leagues when it came to having the influence and capital behind them to pioneer innovations in rocket technology. To say I was fascinated was an understatement.

Long after Sam Branson moved on to chat to others, I remained engrossed in conversation with Michiel Mol. Yet things were about to become even more exciting, simply because I happened to be in the right place at the right time. Perhaps one of the biggest stars present that evening was Sir Bob Geldof. I had seen him earlier at the castle, but with his popularity and the VIP guests around him, I had happily taken it all in from a distance. As soon as Geldof stepped into the lobby, I sensed that people wanted to move in and be seen with him.

My Irish luck was running high that evening. Sir Bob Geldof made his way over to Michiel Mol. They gave each other a hearty embrace and laughed about some previous encounter. Then Michiel introduced me to 'Sir Bob', which made me feel like a million dollars. I couldn't have been more thrilled. I didn't hear what Geldof whispered to Michiel, but it seemed that the after party at the hotel wasn't his scene. They exchanged a few words and it sounded as if they were going to head off somewhere else. Oh well, it had been fun while it lasted. I was already looking around to see who else I could talk to, when Michiel leant over and asked if I'd like to join him and Sir Bob for a drink at a pub they knew. Yes, of course, who needed this crowd anyway!

Geldof, Michiel Mol and I slipped out of the hotel. By this time, the rain was bucketing down and being near the coast, a blustery wind jostled us around, as if being wet was not good enough. I wasn't sure where we were off to, but Geldof knew Dublin and led the way. We zigzagged along some back streets and happened upon a quiet, cosy-looking pub with warm lights on inside.

The bartender was a burly old gentleman with a typically warm-hearted Irish soul. He welcomed us to his cosy little pub. Within moments of finding a spot, we each received a pint of the best Guinness in town. Making her way from the back, the bartender's wife, a woman with the most pronounced Irish accent, brought some snacks. She obviously knew Geldof and they shared a joke about preferring London to his old home town in Ireland.

I couldn't have dreamed of a more perfect situation. I was sitting in a warm pub on the banks of the Liffey River, icy rain pelting down on the cobbled streets outside, far from the madding crowd, drinking Guinness with two absolute characters. One of them was a billionaire space explorer and the other, promising to be his first space tourist, was an Irish singer-songwriter, author and political activist. For all of Geldof's eccentricities, he was always switched on and highly educated on the issues he was passionate about. We spoke at length about Africa, his work with Live-Aid and Mandela's immense contribution to humanity. We shared personal stories of our interactions with Mandela and as if preaching to the converted, affirmed Mandela's global role as a phenomenal leader, negotiating with presidents to affect change and effective leadership.

Long into the night we kept the fires of our imagination burning with ideas, answers to complex problems, experiences and funny stories. For that one night, it didn't matter who I was or how I came to find myself in that tiny pub. We were just a couple of guys out and about, sharing jokes, drinking Ireland's finest, laughing and having a good time.

I doubt that I could ever find that pub again if I returned to Dublin. Like so many of the significant places I have been in my life, they have become the settings for enduring memories that will live forever in my mind and imagination.

A few days later, as I was checking out of the hotel, Boris Becker appeared next to me at the front desk. I had not forgotten about my question and his promise to tell me what he thought about Roger Federer. So without mentioning any names, I turned to Becker and asked if he had thought about my question. He let out a defeated laugh. He turned to me and lent on the counter.

"Federer is unbelievable. He's the best thing to happen to this sport. He commands respect on and off the court; no-one can touch him."

We shook hands and I watched him exit through the glass doors. A car door opened for him, he slipped inside and was whisked away.

He was gone, but I had my answer.

....

CHAPTER 25

JUNGLE BOOK

*I left the shores of familiarity and discovered that
imagination was real.*

Thirty-six hours after leaving home, I walked out of the main
doors of Bandaranaike International Airport on the outskirts
of Colombo, Sri Lanka. The international aroma of airport
air-conditioning gave way to the choking heat and humidity that
is the glorious island nation of Sri Lanka in May. The monsoon
season on the west coast was well underway. The combination
of rain and heat meant that I found myself literally drinking the
saturated atmosphere. I loved it. Flying via Dubai, with a short
stop-over in the Maldives, I had arrived in Colombo. It was my
first time in this part of the world, and I felt I needed to absorb the
moment, so I crossed the street, turned around and stood there
taking in everything that was happening around me. The morning
traffic, people on bicycles, tuk-tuks, taxis and busses all jostled

for a spot on the chaotic road leading into Colombo. Everywhere I looked were palm trees and plants bursting with life: hibiscus flowers three times their usual size, vines and other odd-looking plants that thrived in this climate. I wasn't even moving and I was sweating. What an amazing adventure awaited me over the next few weeks.

Arugam Bay lies directly east of Colombo, some 225km away on the other side of the island. I was meeting a friend there who had arrived two days earlier and was already living it up, surfing and exploring the dry side of the island. I couldn't get there fast enough. Trains were slow and buses were the last option for me. I had scribbled the name of a local airline company on a piece of paper before leaving home. They had promised via e-mail that they could take me across the island to Arugam Bay within 30 minutes. They operated out of an old military base adjoining the airport. Apparently, the flight I needed left at around 11am so I had time. With my backpack, I set off on foot up the road, searching for the sign post for Cinnamon Airways.

Not far up the road, a large government signpost indicated the direction to the military base. Just below this was a happy purple sign, indicating that my odd little airline lay in the same direction.

I haven't been on many military air force bases before, but this one was astonishly beautiful. From the main road, I turned left and entered a wide road canopied by massive flamboyant trees in full bloom, displaying their bright orange flowers. Underneath those trees wafted the perfume of the frangipani tree, also in full bloom. A boom gate stretched across the road, which I guessed marked the entrance to the military base. A quick page through my passport and a friendly wave and I was on my way. Right at the very end, through an old barbwire fence, was a sign that read 'Cinnamon Airways'. I felt as if I was back in Africa. I greeted a friendly woman hiding behind the counter. She opened an old, well-used book, thumbed her fingers through a few pages and then confirmed,

"Ah yes, Willman, Arugam Bay. Welcome, sir." The lady scribbled out a note, placed it in my passport and handed it back to me. "Your pilots will come collect you when they ready."

With that she said goodbye and disappeared through the back door.

I was on my own, so I put my bags down under a table and walked around the place. I didn't have to wait long before two pilots appeared through the barbwire fence. They were laughing about something or other. We greeted. One was British and the other a local Sri Lankan. They grabbed a few papers off the counter and made their way out onto the tarmac.

They both laughed again and turning around, called for me to follow. Surely I wasn't the only passenger that morning? Apparently I was, so I grabbed my stuff and ran to the waiting plane.

I have no idea what kind of plane it was, but instead of wheels it had big pontoons. On closer inspection, I made out wheels under the pontoons.

"Why do we need those things?" I asked, pointing to the pontoons.

"Oh, that's in case we need to land on water. This island doesn't have many landing strips. But don't worry, we're heading to Batticaloa; they have a nice long airstrip there."

Batticaloa was some 100km north of Aragum Bay. I was promised that a taxi would pick me up and take me down the coast.

Within 20 minutes we were off. The plane bounced and shook as it made its way up through the clouds. A quick 30 minute flight and then a 100km taxi ride didn't sound too bad.

Without warning, the plane lurched hard to the right and dived down through the huge bulbous clouds before levelling off. One of the pilots up front apologised.

"Are you in a hurry, sir?"

"Not really, but why have we changed direction?"

"We've just received notice that the President of Sri Lanka is flying across the island, heading straight towards us. We are not allowed to be in this airspace or at this altitude, so we'll have to head south and go around the island, before heading back up to Batticaloa."

"How long will it extend our flight time?"

"Oh, not too much longer; maybe an hour in total."

I was fine with that, so I relaxed again.

After a while, I noticed that we were flying really low, so I asked if it was necessary to fly so low, literally just above the palm trees.

"Oh yes, sorry. Colombo Headquarters radioed, instructing us to pick up two passengers in Dikwella."

Just as he finished explaining, his co-pilot swung out wide over a lagoon and pointed the nose across the water. We were coming in for my first water landing. I didn't even have a chance to speak before the nose lifted and the pontoons slapped the water. The whole plane lurched forward, the front propeller whipping up a storm of water. I couldn't see anything out of the window and then, just like that, we were floating along, headed for a jetty on the edges of a palm-fringed shoreline.

After a quick stop to pick up a couple from Singapore, we were on our way again. The pilots apologised to the couple that they had to drop me off before heading back to Colombo. We bumped along the water for ages before lifting off over the rim of the palm forest and into the big, blue skies. Unlike the relatively smooth flight down to Dikwella, this trip up north was crazy. We jumped around that sky, hitting air pockets, lurching forward, pulling sideways; we held on for dear life. We eventually landed in Batticaloa, but the atmosphere had changed. I was in a foul mood; the Singaporean couple were dead quiet, sweating in the back corner. Man, that was a rough flight.

We hit the dust track like an angry hornet and buzzed around, back towards a tiny shack on the other end of the runway before the pilot killed the engines. The door flipped open and, true to their word, there waiting to welcome us, was one jolly looking Sri Lankan cab driver standing next to his black taxi. I thanked the pilots, jumped into the car and we were off.

Much of my time in Arugam Bay was spent in the warm waters of the Indian Ocean. When I wasn't on the beach, I was out exploring the endless farmlands that line the only road around the island. The heat didn't let up once. At night we lay sprawled out on our beds, sweating, and during the heat of the day we found a palm tree on the beach and carried on sleeping. At around 3pm the heat abated just a bit, which gave us enough energy to go and do something. Bored with watching people surf, I hired a bicycle and headed out along the main road to the next town of Pottuvil.

Just past the town, were vast rice paddies. In the late evenings, it was beautiful. Finding the first dust track off the main road, I'd head out, cycling along, waving at villagers on their way home from their day out in the fields. All the roads were built above the fields. Even though monsoon season was lashing the west coast of Sri Lanka, the east coast was having its dry season. Crossing over tiny bridges, I'd look down at the pools infested with crocodiles. Water buffalo gathered in herds along the water's edge. It was remarkable that these animals looked so similar to the buffalo back home, but were relatively tame. I parked my bike up against an old tree not far off the dust track, and climbed up to the first branch to sit and watch whatever was happening across the flood plains.

It wasn't long before I was rewarded with one of the most intimate experiences of wildlife you could ask for. Coming out of the forest, I caught a glimpse of my first Asian Elephant. At first, only one large, gentle creature emerged. Then suddenly, perhaps forty or more of these giants emerged from the forest on their way to the water's edge. The tree I was sitting in lay between them and the water, so I knew I could potentially be in trouble. In Africa, there would be no way I'd find myself up a tree with a herd of approaching elephant. I had no choice but to lie flat on the branch, which wasn't more than 5 meters off the ground.

Sensing my presence, the matriarch ventured slowly forward. The herd lined up behind her, ever cautious but determined to reach the water in the 40-degree heat. I lay pressed flat on that branch as all forty elephants came right past the tree, not more than 10 meters from me. It was like a scene out of *The Jungle Book*. Everything that Rudyard Kipling had created in his book was right in front of me. If you were patient and allowed nature to reveal itself, you were rewarded with an abundance of creatures. I was fascinated not only by the elephants, but by the number of peacocks that stuck close by the elephant. I don't think Kipling actually needed much imagination: he would only have needed to do exactly what I was doing. Cycling back to Arugam, I had to stop just before an old foot bridge. The entire bridge was festooned with well over two hundred Langur monkeys. Never in my life had I seen so many monkeys cavorting and basically creating havoc as they used the bridge as their path back into the jungle. Whilst watching the monkeys, I peered down underneath the bridge to see huge crocodiles lying in wait for one wrong move by a monkey above. Everything I had read in Kipling's book about these animals living together was real! Everything was too beautiful and idyllic.

It was long after sunset, and I was still a few miles away from the main road. Panic began to set in. I had no light to guide my path, but what I feared more was the realisation that there was also danger out here. Somewhere in that jungle was Shere Khan. After all, Yala Game Reserve was in the distance and this was tiger country. Suddenly, this friendly-looking landscape became menacing. I was comforted whenever I passed the odd villager. I didn't stop to greet anyone; I peddled on as fast as I could. An hour later, I was freewheeling into Arugam Bay in the darkness, the warm air in my hair, my shirt soaked with sweat, but the thrill of adventure alive and well in my heart.

Our accommodation on the beach was in simple wooden houses with a single bed, side desk and mosquito net in each room. I learnt on the first night that leaving any food out was asking for trouble. With the suffocating heat at night we became lazy; we didn't care how exposed we were. I must have been asleep only a few hours, when I felt something touch my foot, or rather brush over my foot. It had been enough to wake me, but after a while I nodded off back to sleep. The second time I woke, I knew that something wasn't right. Whatever was in my room had run over my chest and legs. I was awake immediately. I could hear something moving about in the room. The noise was now coming from a number of places in the room and I could hear whatever it was running over my bed. I slowly picked up my cellphone and shone the light from the screen down the length of my bed. Looking back at me spread out across my bed, on the curtains and side table were literally hundreds of rats. They were everywhere. I let out a kind of bark, something to scare the rodents. It worked: flying off my bed, dropping off the walls and curtains, the rats scattered. I couldn't believe what was happening and in desperation, I eventually found the bedroom light on the wall next to the bed. The rats had torn apart a packet of food I had placed on the table. All I was concerned about was whether any of the rats had bitten me. Knowing that rats can carry disease, I took a shower and scrubbed myself whilst carefully looking for any bite marks. I stripped my bed of its sheets, threw away any food and hung up the mosquito net. I literally cocooned myself in that net.

A few hours later, they were back in my room, clambering up and down my mosquito net, but I had done a good job of insulating myself. It was still unnerving having them crawling all over, but they weren't able to get through the netting.

The next day, I bought toilet paper and poison. Using these, I made a thick soup in the basin and plastered up any hole, crack or gap that could possibly allow the rats back into my room. I was in luck; it worked. Initially, I could hear the rats going crazy, scratching away, trying to bite through the poisoned papier-mâché, but by the third night it was dead quiet. They were either dead or had pushed off to torment someone else. Of course, the owner of the chalets denied there were any rats at all!

Travelling back to Colombo, we took the train. For three days, we travelled through the mountainous areas of central Sri Lanka. We enjoyed two nights staying over in the most beautiful tea plantations along the way. From the mountains, our train wound its way down through some of the most beautiful forests I have ever laid eyes on. It was as if time stood still; as if Mowgli himself had escaped to these tiny villages and lived out his adventures in these very forests.

....

CHAPTER 26

IN GRATITUDE

"It's a funny thing about life, once you begin to take note of the things you are grateful for, you begin to lose sight of the things that you lack."   **- Germany Kent**

As you can imagine, Nelson Mandela was, for anyone with extreme wealth, power or influence, the man you had to be seen with. Without fail, a famous person would jet into South Africa, spend a day on Robben Island and the next day fly to Johannesburg for an audience with Mandela. Sometimes it seemed as if all that mattered in South Africa was Robben Island and Nelson Mandela. If you took note of global politics it was easy to anticipate. Whenever a world leader needed to improve his or her public image, they would come to see Mandela. I used to joke on Facebook that whenever I had a shoot with Mandela, I was "off to see the Wizard."

On many of those occasions, I was waiting in Madiba's lounge to be called through into his office for a quick photo shoot with Madiba and his guest. I certainly wasn't called to shoot every person that came through, but over the years I've had the opportunity to share a few special moments with some truly fascinating people.

Every shoot had its protocols and a set out structure. We all knew the drill. In the beginning, I found myself guessing what would happen next, but as I grew familiar with the set-up it all became second nature. There was an order to how things happened and, if you were sharp in reading the dynamics of the day, you might even be given more opportunities or time to shoot.

I would arrive well ahead of the scheduled time. I'd check in with those controlling the day's events, get the low down and then go about preparing on my own. Before Mandela or anyone arrived, I'd go through to Madiba's office to check the lighting and make sure there was enough space for me to work. The event itself generally happened so quickly, that there was hardly ever really any time to take it all in. At most, I had 10 or 15 minutes to capture the images before being politely ushered out of the office.

I always regarded Madiba's office as the inner sanctum, a kind of 'ground zero', a space so respected and revered that only a few privileged people were allowed the opportunity to enter. There was a certain stillness about the space. The thick carpets, heavy curtains and bullet-proof windows cocooned the room from the outside world. You could spend your life working at the Mandela Foundation and never go through to Mandela's office. It was at the end of a long corridor, well away from the day-to-day offices and visitors to the Foundation. I've never been to the Oval Office in the White House, so I can't compare them but if it is anything like Madiba's office, it must be a special place.

The half hour or so before Madiba arrived, I would be in the office, preparing things. Generally, I was allowed to enter without a bodyguard or staff member escorting me. I appreciated the trust and made sure that I didn't do anything to cause concern. The most precious thing about those times was the privilege of standing alone with my camera at my side, soaking it all in. It was dead quiet in there and for a few minutes I would look at Madiba's chair or desk or simply wander into his lounge and allow my imagination to recall previous shoots and funny moments.

During one shoot, things were progressing slowly. Madiba had been receiving guests the whole morning. I had been in the office with him for a few hours already. It was quite a process for Zelda and her assistants to bring in a guest, who would sit with Madiba for 10 minutes and then be led out. Many of the guests that day were very old, which gave me plenty of time to sit in the corner and enjoy what I was experiencing. Madiba was sitting in the corner of the lounge in his usual wing-back chair. This made it easy for guests to approach him and then to sit for a few photos together before chatting one on one.

I was up against one of the windows that looked out across the garden of the Mandela Foundation and over a brick wall onto the M1 freeway, which runs the length of one side of the Foundation property. Inside, the atmosphere was very peaceful; we were all enjoying our time with Madiba. Outside it was hot and midmorning traffic on the freeway was busy. The bulletproof glass gave everything outside a slight green tint. I often wondered if anyone in those cars ever knew that behind the thick glass was Madiba, sitting in the lounge of his large office.

As the years rolled by, many individuals from all walks of life came through the double doors of Madiba's office. It was lovely to see how people reacted when they walked into the office and found Madiba waiting to greet them. Those who had never met him before generally reacted in a state of awe and disbelief. You could feel their excitement. I never met with the guests in the anteroom before they came into the office, so my first interaction with them was at the moment they entered. They themselves never took photos as it was understood that the Mandela Foundation would make sure images from the meeting with Madiba would be sent to them formally. This eliminated awkward moments and definitely stopped people using flash photography around Madiba.

To all these guests, I was merely a fly on the wall. I was there to do a good job without drawing any attention to myself. I didn't speak, and guests generally seemed to know what to expect. With the meet and greet and the formal group photo taken, I was out of there. After a short while, the guests would re-emerge. They would then either be given a tour of the Foundation or shake hands with members of the staff and leave. If it was a guest I really liked, I made sure to stand in line to shake their hand before disappearing myself.

It never really dawned on me that what I was doing deserved any thanks. I always felt that it was as much a privilege for me to be there, as it was for them. I was all too aware that, within a few hours, I would be back home in Durban, out of the bubble that surrounded Mandela, getting on with my life. So many people had come and gone over the years that I had become familiar with the routine.

It took one woman to step out of the protective bubble, to make me feel appreciated and realise that the work I was doing had true value.

I arrived at the Foundation to learn that a delegation from the Government of India would be visiting Mandela that morning. Leading the state visit was the President of the Indian National Congress Party, Sonja Gandhi, accompanied by many of her party's ministers. As head of the ruling party, she was entitled to be Prime Minister but had chosen not to be. She was of Italian descent and the widow of the former Prime Minister, Rajiv Gandhi. She felt that taking on the role of Prime Minister would lead to bloodshed and possible attempts at assassination. However, as head of the party in power, she enjoyed all the benefits.

I remember how crazy the whole morning was. I was glad to slip into Madiba's office, away from the general buzz of expectation. Sonja Gandhi's time with Madiba was good. After leaving the room, I waited for their meeting to conclude and for the touring group to exit. I was surprised to see that Madiba himself was accompanying them on their way out. It must have been a very good meeting, as this didn't usually happen. After the farewells, Madiba waved goodbye, turned and headed back into his office. As often happened, the dignitaries prepared to shake hands with various members of staff before making their way out toward the main entrance of the Foundation, where the motorcade was waiting.

Without any warning, Sonja Gandhi made her way over to me and with both hands reached out, took my right hand, and personally thanked me for capturing a few photos of her with Nelson Mandela that morning. She spoke about how thankful she was, and that she would cherish them forever. I don't think anyone, least of all me, had anticipated that. Of all the people who came through those doors during my 10 years at the Foundation, the only person who ever came up to thank me personally was the President of the Indian National Congress Party, Sonja Gandhi. It meant so much to me, that I failed to answer her back with any dignity. I fumbled over my words and stopped short of saying I would fly to India to deliver them to her personally.

Even today, when I have the pleasure of watching Zelda la

Grange and others who worked with Mandela give a speech, I am always warmed to see so much of how Mandela interacted with people reflected in the way they relate to those around them. I see him in small gestures and phrases that they use and it makes me smile.

....

CHAPTER 27

OF SQUIRRELS AND NUTS

I have sat with presidents and paupers. If I am to aspire to great things, I will take heed the words of great men. But if I am to discover my true heart, I will make space for the lowly.

Human nature is resilient, devious, cunning and completely awe-inspiring, all at the same time. Who we are and how we continue to shape and alter ourselves to achieve our goals is truly amazing. We hear incredible stories of people lost in the jungle, relying on their wits to survive. We read accounts of individuals who, through sheer determination, through failure after failure, rise up to create empires in business or art. Sadly, there is also a fallen side to human nature, and when darker forces are at play, our obsessions, frailties and insecurities rise up in attempts to destroy whoever and whatever appears to be in our way. Yet in all this, the cycle of change, adaptation and recreation is what drives us forward.

Cape Town is without doubt one of Africa's jewels. It forms a symbolic island, with wide open deserts to the north and east and the vast South Atlantic Ocean lapping on its southern and western shores. On the southern tip of Africa, protected by a few rugged mountains, lies a city and a people bustling with life. I spent many months looking out over Cape Town from Robben Island, not as a prisoner but as a photographer working on the island. On the furthest point of Robben Island, the side closest to the mainland, there is an old, tired grey-looking building. I have been there many times with former political prisoners or whilst photographing alone. It is a place of stark beauty that would be a perfect retreat with the addition of large decks, umbrellas and warm log fires burning inside during the long inhospitable winter storms that well up from the frigid South Atlantic. But this windswept point, situated where impressive breakers strike thick concrete walls, is testament to a sad history. For it was here that the state's secret police would meet, secure in the knowledge that no-one would overhear their devious plans: a symbol of the darker side of humanity. Miraculously, from this same island mired in almost 400 years of isolation and hatred, would emerge a symbol of the triumph of the human spirit over adversity; a symbol of the nobler side of human nature.

For many years, I had the privilege of documenting the work of the Vodacom Foundation throughout South Africa. For six weeks each year, I immersed myself in documenting the many organisations, 'start-ups' and institutions funded by the Foundation. No two organisations were the same. It was tremendously exciting to gain insight into how the people of South Africa were focusing their efforts to assist less fortunate communities and bring about positive change. It was whilst photographing for the Vodacom Foundation that I witnessed a prime example of the positive side of human nature.

On the slopes below Devil's Peak, on the fringe of the city bowl, lies an organisation focussed on assisting the homeless. We identified a few individuals supported by the centre whom I could work with over a few days. The first was a man in his sixties. He owned nothing in the world except for his two dogs. They were his life. Accompanied by his dogs, he made the entire city his home. He had a freedom and self-assurance not often seen in the homeless. There are very real problems associated with homelessness, and without seeking to glorify the condition, he openly admitted that he had actively chosen and preferred this way of life. Possibly, his earlier life had been very different. I don't believe he was born into this condition. Various life choices and hard-hitting circumstances forced him out onto the streets. Choice is a part of the human dilemma.

The second person I worked with was a woman with a young child, who quite plainly was lost in a cycle of drugs, abuse and prostitution. Her only refuge was this centre. She chose not heed the advice and counsel provided to her at the centre, and I often wonder what became of her and the tiny child she dragged around with her wherever she went.

The third individual, at first scared the heck out of me. We met him not at the centre, but in an old parking lot, early one evening. During the day, the parking lot was filled with cars, but at night it was his territory. As the last cars left the lot around 6pm, the night dwellers moved in. One by one, they came with their cardboard boxes, blankets, plastic sheeting and bags of worldly possessions. I watched from under a small tree as he greeted each fellow homeless person, took money from them and indicated where in the parking lot they could camp for the night. With a large iron rod, dressed in heavy clothing, he stalked around lording it over his slum and the vagrants from all walks of life entering his domain.

The homeless tend to exist in a world parallel to our own. Hiding behind our own insecurities and paying little attention, allows us to ignore what is actually going on. Turf warfare is rife in these communities. It is often brutal. They see little point in protecting someone else, so it is each vagrant for himself. I tried many times to sit the large man down to talk about his experiences, but he refused. He had travelled a long distance down the tracks from the world that I represented, and he would not allow himself to step back into my world and talk about it in casual conversation.

It was heart-wrenching to travel with the local police force and experience the things they dealt with. At the same time, it was beautiful to witness the care and respect that many of the police officers showed towards the growing community of homeless people in and around the city.

I learnt two months later that my parking lot 'slum-lord' had been shot multiple times in a dispute that erupted one evening on his turf. Out of respect, we decided not to use any of his images in our reports.

I thought I had learnt all there was to learn about homelessness after spending the better part of a week in their company. All that changed on the last day, when I met one of the most lively, sharp and witty people I have ever met.

We met in Rondebosch, on Main Road, a street that runs the length of the southern suburbs of Cape Town. I was standing outside a fast food joint, watching him. As soon as the traffic signal turned red, creating a long line of cars, three lanes deep, this character emerged to do his thing between the waiting cars. He was perhaps in his mid-thirties, thin as a rake, making his living in the most unconventional way. He still wore the iconic "No food, No clothes, No place to sleep" sign, but he also washed car windows and performed a few tricks.

After perhaps thirty minutes of working his turf in-between the cars, he took a break. The morning traffic was thinning out, so he came over to us. He knew one of the social workers from the centre and was all smiles, greeting us with much fanfare. We all introduced ourselves. With his familiar Cape accent made even more pronounced by the lack of his two front teeth, he was out to impress. Treating me as another motorist and a potential 'giver', he launched into a few poems he had made up. They were amazing. In one breath, he rapped out 200 words about life on the street and his favourite BMW motorcar, mixed with fruit salad recipes and Mandela the hero. It was fascinating. *How was it that a young man such as this, homeless, out of work, who lived on the periphery of society, with a life expectancy of only a few more years, had gotten into such a situation?* I wanted to sit him down, and get him something proper to eat so we could talk, but he wouldn't have it. In his rapping, rhyming kind of reply he said that he had to head across town quickly to work another street for a few hours. Time was money and he had to go. But he did say he'd be back at the same spot later in the day, to work the afternoon traffic. With that, he disappeared.

True to his word, at 4pm he was back, sporting a change of clothes and a whole new performance for the tired motorists on their way home after a long day's work. This time, he approached the drivers' windows and told a joke or said something funny. Once again, I was in awe of his ability. But, oh my word, did he earn his money! Not everyone gave money or acknowledged him, but most did. For two hours, he did his act. With his day's work over, he sauntered back over to us with a cheeky smile and a confident swagger. He knew he had been on form out there, working 'his' traffic.

This time, he allowed me some time to chat. *Where should I even begin?* I wanted to know where he stayed. His answer was quick and to the point. Anywhere he wished. *Where does he leave his clothes whilst he is out and about working the streets?* In bags, usually in bushes or unused rubbish bins. *Had he ever made the mistake of putting his belongings somewhere, only to return and find that the municipality had cleared the area or cleaned out the bins?* A whole trail of foul words came forth which answered my question pretty clearly. Yes, a few times!

Without asking too many questions, I knew from his manner-isms, the way he spoke, his age and brief answers that this guy was a survivor, living on the edge, doing his best to make things happen. I had no doubt he either carried a gun or knife. Life was dangerous on the streets. I admired the fact that he never allowed himself to be dragged into discussing the negative reality of his life and circumstances. He avoided disclosing anything that would force him to admit that there was a better way in life. He knew he had intellectual abilities beyond those he was using, but with no-one looking out for him, he had resolved to be content in a narrowly-focussed life.

"Are you any good at counting?" I asked.

His reply was,

"How much you got?"

"What do you mean, how much have I got?"

"Ja, my bru, how much geld you got on you?"

I fished out about thirty-five rand and showed it to him.

"You gotta credit card, ek sê?"

"No, not on me now."

"So, you see, I'm richer than you right now. You got 35 bucks, but I got a lot more."

"On you?" I enquired.

"Everywhere!" he replied, pretending not to be interested in me, looking out across the street as if he had to continually check who was on his turf.

"I don't understand. You must earn some good money doing your gig on the streets every day; do you have a bank account?"

"Naai man, what's wrong wit you? Can't you see I'm homeless? What will those banks do with me? They'll just steal everything I got. Nee, my bra, they just thieves."

"Okay, so where do you keep your money?"

"Flippen hells, bra, you ask a lot of questions!" Again, he refused to look at me, but continued to stare out across the street, his eyes darting back and forth.

"Sorry, but you're my new hero, after what I saw today. I just want to know that you're okay."

He didn't reply; we just sat there on the curb, me looking at him and him looking out at some far, distant point. I wasn't sure what was in his mouth, but he was playing with something. It looked like an old toothpick. Whatever it was, it caused him to make frequent sucking noises.

"Tell me, how do you spend your money?" I asked, keen to get an answer out of him.

"I spend it!"

"On what? I replied quickly.

"Brandy. Only the best."

"And the rest of your money?"

Again, he was silent. For the first time, he looked at me.

"Where you from?"

"Durban, far away from here. So, don't worry, we'll never meet again."

"Ja, bra, you check those small animals there by Parliament Gardens, there by the cathedral?"

"Yes, I know the place. Why?"

"Have you ever sat there, watching those rats?"

"You mean the squirrels that beg for food from people walking past?"

"Exactly; those rats with the big tails."

"Yes, I've seen them."

"You check how they grab what's what and run off?"

"Yes. They dash back into the bush and either eat what they've been given or hide it away."

"Exactly!" He slapped his thigh as if I'd finally cottoned on to what he was saying.

"Ja, so what?" I replied.

"You see this street?"

"What, this one, Main Road?"

"Ja, this street we in – this is my bank." I didn't say anything. I wanted him to continue. "Me, I'm like those furry rats you call squirrels. I got money buried all over this city. Even here, I got stashes of money all over and you wouldn't even know where."

I let out a loud laugh.

"Are you being serious? So, you're saying that right here somewhere near us, you've hidden money?"

"Ay, don't laugh, bra, I'm serious. I got cash everywhere. If they attack me and try steal my money, they don' find nutting."

"No ways!"

I didn't know what to say. He had sat and watched those squirrels and decided that the best way to keep his money safe was to hide it.

"How much you reckon you've got?"

"Much more than you have right now."

"What you going to do with it all?"

"Nothing, just gonna keep it."

"Is that what gives you security, living out on the streets?"

He didn't answer.

"Ja, my bru, unless you gonna give me something for helping you, I'm outta here."

With that he jumped up, slapped my hand in a gangster-type manner and was off. The street lights were green and I watched him disappear around the corner, never to see him again.

I've been back to Cape Town many times since that week. I've never seen him doing his thing in the spots he said he worked. Often, I stop my car next to a park or back alley and wonder how much money is stashed away in clever little spots where no-one else can find it. I like to believe that what he said was true and that somewhere out there is a young man living a life of exuberance and creativity, with secret stashes of money that continue to sustain him.

....

CHAPTER 28

IN PASSING

'Do not go gentle into that good night,
Old age should burn and rage at close of day;
Rage, rage against the dying of the light.'
  - Dylan Thomas, In Country Sleep, And Other Poems, 1947

There is never a right time for anything in life. Things just
happen and we face the challenges as bravely as we can.
Sometimes, we get to watch from the side-lines as the story
of life unfolds.

Growing up as a teenager during the final years of apartheid in
South Africa, I felt as if everything, all the change that was going
on, was happening somewhere else, far away from me. I watched
it on a tiny colour television in our lounge. Everything I knew
about the world outside came through that television. None of
it really touched home until the autumn morning of the 27th of
April 1994.

For the first time, on that cool, cloudless morning, all South African citizens over the age of 18 years, were called upon by the government to exercise their right and lawful duty to leave their homes and vote in the country's first fully democratic elections.

I was too young, so come midmorning, I watched as my parents left the house to go to vote. They didn't speak to us kids; they climbed in the car and left. I had no idea if they were ever coming back. I had conjured up in my mind a picture of the absolute mayhem that would ensue as people tried to make their way to the voting stations. We had heard many threats in the days and weeks leading up to the day of elections, promises of violence should the voting go ahead. The only real memory I have of that day, is of me sitting high up in an old syringa-berry tree in the garden, waiting for my parents return.

I remember, a few years before those elections, walking into our corner grocery-store with my mother and looking up at the image of a man on the wall. It had been printed on cheap poster paper by our local newspaper. It was a sketch of a black man's face, but it had been drawn in such a way as to instil fear in anyone who saw it. It was intended to be a likeness of what they suspected Nelson Mandela would look like.

Nelson Mandela was still in prison and for over twenty-seven years, newspapers had been banned from publishing his photograph. In addition, no new images of him had been released since he went to prison. So, the public really had no idea what Mandela would look like. The government-controlled newspapers were therefore at liberty to depict this 'terrorist' in any way they liked. That badly-drawn portrait was the very first time I had ever seen or heard anything about Nelson Mandela.

I had no idea that this man would one day play such a magnificent role in my own life. People walked past; my mother had gone into the shop, but I stood there, transfixed, an 11-year-old boy unaware that I was looking at my future hero for the first time. It would be a further thirteen years before I would actually reach out and shake his hand.

We all knew from the very beginning that there was an urgency to our work, and that our time with Madiba was running out. From the very first photo shoot I did in his lounge, going through old photographs taken of him on Robben Island, we understood that the clock was ticking. During the last few years of Mandela's life, one heard almost weekly of someone who had been a part of his life passing away. In documenting not only Mandela, but also those who had shared his life, we were engaged in a race against eternity; an attempt to record very personal memories, insights and invaluable 'mental archives' before they were lost to us forever.

We were all aware that at some point Mandela himself would leave us, the clock would wind down, leaving us with only our grief and an awareness of the huge role that he had played in each of our lives. But he personally, would exist no more.

I battle even today to reflect on the images I captured during private moments with this man. Perhaps one image stands out more than the others. It comes from a shoot where I had the idea of capturing close up images of Madiba's hand, as he wrote on a piece of paper. The images were focussed and pin-sharp. They revealed an intimacy that had not been seen before: the texture of his skin, how he used nail-clippers to cut his nails, the shape of his fingers, the detailed markings and lines on his hands. They are moving; an intimate treasure trove, beautifully captured. Yet, when I look at them today, I know that those same hands no longer exist; they have vanished and are now a part of the earth on a hillside over-looking the Qunu countryside, Madiba's final place of rest.

I have never been to Mandela's grave. I didn't even go to the funeral. As with all events, there are stories and hidden agendas behind the headlines. When pieced together, these varied perspectives help to develop a bigger picture of what was going on during those momentous days.

Monday morning, 3 December 2013: I was seated on the stage of my old school, as an invited guest for their Speech Day (annual awards ceremony). I had not been back to my old Senior Primary School for twenty years. So little had changed, and I felt that only I had grown older. As a gift to the school, I presented them at the end of the morning with one of my prized portrait works of Nelson Mandela. It was as if everything had come full circle. With so much talk of Mandela being so close to death, I was glad that I had been given the opportunity to share with them a tiny piece of my journey with Mandela while he was still alive.

As soon as the event was over, I raced home to change, grabbed an already packed suitcase, and headed to the airport to catch a flight to Cape Town. That evening I relaxed with friends, sharing stories about the morning's events back in Pinetown. I was surprised at how at peace I was, talking about Mandela. It had been a while since I last saw him, but for some reason, having shared a little with my old school, and with new work and experiences taking shape in my life, I felt ready to let Madiba go. I had played my part and was moving on to new things.

There was much drama during Mandela's final years. The government kept making 'reassuring' statements on his condition, using words like 'Mandela is critical but stable' or was it 'stable but critical'? Either way, nothing made sense. Then we heard news of how the ambulance he was travelling in had broken down on the way to hospital!

Every time Mandela was admitted to hospital, the world press declared that this was it, we must be prepared to receive news that he had died. Yet, after every visit to hospital, Madiba recovered and was taken back home. Panic over.

All this had gone on for months on end. I remember, after the first major health-scare, I received a call from a friend who worked in the higher ranks of the African National Congress. I was out at dinner and she called to say that 'the President's people were making their way to Mandela's house'. This, of course, raised alarm bells at first, but after putting the phone down, I had an inkling that it was a false alarm. No-one in the Mandela family had said anything to me, and the Mandela Foundation hadn't given word of any imminent passing. So I went back to my dinner party and carried on as if nothing had happened. Indeed, nothing happened … for 18 months.

During Mandela's long illness, I was in and out of contact with the Mandela Foundation. I don't recall ever asking anyone how Mandela was. I knew that if things grew worse, I'd get wind of it.

Sadly, not long after the trips back and forth to hospital, images appeared on television and in the newspapers of Mandela being visited by then President of South Africa, Mr Jacob Zuma. The world gasped at how frail Mandela was. He was lifeless and didn't move at all. He sat there expressionless, while the president and his group of visitors capered around him, posing for pictures. I was disgusted and became angry that this type of thing had been allowed to happen. The government reported that the president had made a courtesy call on the aging Mr Mandela, and that the president had reported that Mandela was well and in good spirits. Nothing in those photos suggested anything but death and gloom as people jostled to be seen with Mandela. What enraged me even more was that the unknown people who had accompanied the president had used cellphone cameras and flashes to take 'selfies'. This showed both total disrespect and a lack of awareness that

Madiba's eyes could not handle the intensity of flash photography. *Where was Zelda? Who was handling protocol that morning?* It was clearly a publicity stunt of the lowest order.

Why had this happened? Who was protecting Madiba? Zelda would never have allowed this to happen. *Where was Madiba's wife, Graça Machel?*

I later learnt that no-one had been there to protect Madiba on that shameful day. Graça Machel, as far as I could tell, had been away on business at the time. I knew that Madiba's house-manager and house staff would not have dared to prevent the president and his people from visiting. I recognised a few family members in the photos too, which only increased my disappointment about the whole episode. This sad event reinforced my belief that Madiba would have suffered more abuse and died much sooner if Zelda had not been there with such a fierce and determined commitment to protect and care for Madiba for all those years.

On Wednesday, the 4th of December, I was out and about working in Cape Town. I had been across to Archbishop Desmond Tutu's Foundation that day to meet with a few people and had started work in Khayelitsha informal settlement on the Cape Flats.

By Thursday the 5th of December, I had forgotten about the first few days of the week and was fully engrossed in my work in and around Cape Town. The weather had been spectacular, and that evening I met up with friends out in Kalk Bay. We enjoyed an early dinner and I was home and in bed just after 9pm.

I must have dozed off quickly, because around 10pm I sat up abruptly to the sound of my phone ringing. I thought it was my alarm, so I shut it off. I curled back up, content that I wouldn't be disturbed again. Not a minute later, the phone went off again. This time I sat up, put on the bedside light and saw that it was actually a phone call. The number was from Johannesburg. If this was a wrong number, I was going to blast them for calling so late.

In a gruff voice I answered the call.

"Hello Matthew, its Getty Images here."

"Getty Images? Why are you calling me so late?"

"Oh, haven't you heard?"

"Heard what?"

"Mandela passed away not more than an hour ago. We want to know if we have your permission to release the images that we obtained from the Nelson Mandela Foundation."

"Matthew, are you there? Hello … Matthew? Hello Matthew, can we release the images?"

"Yes …" I cleared my throat, "Yes, please do …" I hung up.

I sat in bed, looking out of the window. I had forgotten to draw the curtains, so I sat there in the dark, staring out into more darkness. Madiba was gone.

I didn't know what to do at first. I knew that if this was true, then there would be people at the Mandela Foundation working throughout the night to co-ordinate things.

I was staying with a friend in Bishopscourt that week. We were actually house-sitting a beautiful home with impressive views onto the mountains. I needed to check what the news-reports were saying, so I made my way down to the lounge, found the TV remote and flicked through channels to find the news. The first to pop up was BBC, who were already marking Mandela's passing. Channel after news channel: CNN, Al Jazeera News and our local TV stations, SABC and E-News were all reporting that Mandela had passed away. It was true. I stood there absorbing the news. I hadn't anticipated the moment when I would learn of his passing. I was in a state of utter disbelief.

I went to wake my friend. She flung a few words of irritation at me until I explained what was going on. We both stood in front of the TV, watching everything unfold. Without a word, the kettle was switched on; lights were turned on in the lounge, kitchen and dining-room. There was a long night ahead. I had work to do.

I ran back upstairs, changed back into my clothes, grabbed my laptop and made a place for myself in the dining-room where I could work and still see what was happening on the television in the next room.

Hour after hour, I received e-mails forwarded on from various parties, institutions, businesses and charities, asking for permission to use my images for their own condolences or news reports. That night, I received e-mails from Mexico, India, Australia, America and Europe. Getty Images, who had woken me up to this new reality, were copying me in on who they were sending my images out to. I put my phone on silent, as my friend had gone back to bed, but only after making sure I was well-stocked with food, snacks and lots of tea.

Around 5am the next morning, having worked through the night, still numb to the actual reality that Madiba was no longer with us, I flopped into bed. I had to be back at work in the townships at 9am, so I was hoping to get at least three hours of sleep.

Just before 6am, my phone rang. It was Lavinia Crawford-Brown, Archbishop Desmond Tutu's personal assistant. We exchanged a few kind words and then she asked if I was still in Cape Town, because 'The Arch' was making his way to St George's Cathedral in Wale Street, Cape Town, to say a special mass. Was I interested in attending? Absolutely, I wouldn't miss it for the world.

Most of Cape Town was only starting to wake to the news of Mandela's passing as I headed up over de Waal Drive into the city centre.

Along the side of the Cathedral, I found a pew which gave me a perfect vantage point to be a part of the proceedings but also to remain hidden. News had spread quickly that the Archbishop was doing a service. By the end of the service, a number of people who had been on their way to work had made time to come in and be a part of the small church service. The media were there, of course, with their lights and clattering cameras.

It was very moving to watch Desmond Tutu use the occasion to call us all to reflect on what he called "the magnanimity of Mandela's life," to celebrate a life so well-lived. I truly felt that if there was a ground zero on the morning after Mandela's passing, it was right there with Archbishop Desmond Tutu, and not at Mandela's house in Johannesburg or the Mandela Foundation. It was as if the moral authority had been passed on to Archbishop Tutu, now that Mandela was no longer with us.

I was doing well until the church organ played a rendition of our national anthem, *Nkosi, Sikelel' iAfrika*. I sat in the pew and cried. Maybe I was too tired to do anything else. Whilst still pulling myself together and with the service over, I joined Lavinia Crawford-Brown and Archbishop Tutu near the side sacristy of the cathedral and we talked. I remember Lavinia telling the Archbishop that I had worked with Mandela for many years, and I remember Tutu clasping his hands together and saying, in his typically exuberant voice,

"Ooh, that's marvellous."

We laughed, but all three of us felt the weight of the occasion. All we could do was smile and reminisce.

I committed that day to going into the township of Khayelitsha to work. I wanted to feel the mood of the people out there, those whose lives Mandela had touched the most. While I was doing my thing, photographing and interacting with the people, my phone rang. It was the producer of E-News back in Cape Town. She asked if I would be prepared to be on the lunch-time show at their studios in the city. I agreed and a short while later, I drove back into the city.

The whole building was a frenzy of activity, news was coming in thick and fast, people were lining up to be interviewed and have their say. I went through to the studio, was mic'd up and made my way to the spot where the presenter was standing-by. It was only then that it dawned on me that this media machine was broadcasting out live across Africa, and that people were relying on them to learn more about this historic occasion. What really surprised me was that in front of me, former president FW de Klerk was on air along with other notable South African personalities. The broadcast took a break, allowing the current panel to leave. We all stood in the 'green room' together; I shook Mr de Klerk's hand and we spoke briefly before being told that I needed to take my seat on set.

So much of that day was just a blur. I loved how everyone was rallying together, sharing stories, making statements about Mandela and there I was, without any pressure or expectations, in the middle of it all. Of all the questions that the presenter asked me that day, one question truly had an impact on those in the studio. I was asked what I could say to the audiences at this point in history about Mandela. It was not a question I needed to think about, the answer had already taken root within me:

"I am not a president or a person of influence. I merely served the needs of the Mandela Foundation, which afforded me many intimate moments with Mr Mandela, and I can say this about him: the man we all came to love and see in public on TV or radio, I can affirm that this was the same man I came to appreciate in private. Mandela was the same both publically and privately, and I honestly believe that to be the truth, and we can all take strength in knowing that."

I could sense the presenter had loved that reply; her mood warmed immediately and she allowed herself to reveal a little of her own emotions at that moment.

Later that afternoon, I returned to the house in Bishopscourt. I needed to take a nap and gather my thoughts. The e-mails and telephone calls had died down. I had done my duty. I had made sure that I had given what was needed of me. I spent that weekend with friends. My mood wasn't heavy; in fact, I was quite numb to it all. It was only the following Monday, around mid-morning, that I found a quiet spot and rang my boss at the Mandela Foundation, just to chat. It was a strange conversation. I had rarely, if ever, allowed myself to be personal or show emotion, but here I was talking to Verne as if he was an old friend. We both agreed that it was all a bit lonely. We were functioning as we should, doing our part, but it was such a significant time and I felt isolated. Verne very kindly told me to fly up to Johannesburg and come and hang out at the Foundation and help out wherever I could. They had a lot on their hands. He even laughed, saying I could help handle all the flowers they were receiving.

I agreed I'd go, but later in the day, I decided that it was not my place. I wanted to watch this whole drama from the side-lines. I didn't want to be at the core of where it was all happening. Over the next few days, I watched the Mandela family all coming out and being interviewed. I watched TV crews filming in all the places I had spent years documenting and working before they'd been open to the public and celebrated by the Mandela Foundation. I didn't want to be a part of the hype. I had nothing more to say. If I'm honest, I wasn't important enough to be heard. My images were doing their job where they were needed. Those images were my contribution; they expressed my heart and would speak far more eloquently than I could.

Over the days that followed, I was amazed to see so many newspapers printing my portraits of Mandela on their front pages. I wasn't sure how it made me feel. I had worked privately for many years to get those images. Few people had seen my images of Mandela, and yet here they were, front and centre, displayed for all to see, as the world's attention focussed on Mandela and the life he had led.

We all knew that there was still the funeral to get through. Over the course of the following week, so many people asked me whether I was going to go. I had no idea who was being given accreditation and who wasn't. Mid-week I phoned Mandla Mandela, Madiba's eldest grandson, once we had learnt from the government the date of the funeral in Qunu. Our conversation was light-hearted. Mandla said it would be wonderful to have me attend the funeral, but that he couldn't give me accreditation himself. All accreditation was being handled by the office of the Presidency at the Union Buildings in Pretoria, and one had to appear in person. I learnt that no-one from the Mandela Foundation had been invited to attend, which was shocking and a clear indication of the discord between the government and those who had served Madiba and strived to preserve his legacy.

The next day, I watched as Mandla Mandela stood beside the open casket of his grandfather, as thousands and thousands of ordinary South Africans filed past to pay their final respects. It just so happened that while I was watching, the cameras focused in on a very familiar face, Zelda, Madiba's personal assistant. Like the rest of the country, she too had to stand in long queues, as if she had never met the man or had no direct connection with him. I watched as she filed past the coffin. It was heart-breaking. Tears welled up in my eyes as I saw her break down, leaning heavily on the shoulders and arms of those who were with her. It must have been a horrific and incredibly painful thing to experience. How do you go from working so intimately with a man, knowing everything about him, his hopes and fears, to getting only a few seconds to say goodbye in such a public manner? It was devastating to see. It was only once I took my eyes off Zelda, that I recognised who was with her and doing his best to support her. It was none other than Bono, the lead singer of the band, U2. I am sure he must have been a tremendous support to her. Watching all this play out on the television, I realised that it was much bigger than me. I had no place expecting to play any part during this time. So, I resigned myself to staying away and going through the motions on my own. It was a good decision. In the end, it allowed me to deal with my feelings privately, without being publicly analysed, required to act in a certain way or say the correct thing.

The saddest moment was watching Madiba's flag-draped coffin being placed in the military aeroplane at Waterkloof Air Force Base. I stood in silence as I watched the plane taxi to the runway, and watched Madiba leaving Pretoria and Johannesburg for the last time. I kept thinking back to around 2004, when Madiba shared with us how, as a young man, he had run away from the abaThembu regent at the time, to make a new life for himself in the bustling city of Johannesburg. That had been in the 1940s and now, here I was, witnessing him leaving this heart of Africa for the last time. It was very, very heavy.

Finally, the time came for Madiba to be buried, on a hillside in Qunu, under the bright African sun, in the baked earth that he had loved. I watched, standing in my tiny lounge, crying as I saluted the visuals being broadcast. To anyone watching, I would have looked like a complete idiot, saluting the television. But in the same manner that I had promised to always wear a suit in the presence of Madiba, no matter where I was, I accorded him the respect and dignity of honouring him one final time, as his body was returned to the earth. I didn't have to be there. I didn't have to be around anyone. My actions were a part of my own journey. They were a personal tribute. As a child, I had gazed up at a news-paper poster taped to a grocery store door and feared the man depicted there, a man I didn't know or understand. Since then, I had come to know that man better and discovered that he was a subtle mentor, an encourager and a man who transformed lives.

I don't know if I will ever go to the grave of Nelson Mandela. If I do, it will only be after many years have passed. I don't need to have closure by going to his grave. For me that closure came from what turned out to be the last time I ever saw Nelson Mandela alive.

On that final day, my photo-shoot with Madiba had ended. Taking Graça's hand, he rose from his wing-back chair. Next to him was one of his oldest friends, a man who had walked along-side him during his twenty-seven years in prison and been his co-accused at the Rivonia trial, Mr Ahmed Kathrada. Together, they walked across Madiba's private office, towards his waiting car, outside the door.

Still smiling and making comments about his advanced age, Madiba slowly made his way out of his office. He smiled at me and Verne Harris standing to one side, and breathed the air of his post-presidential office one last time. In this office, he had met with guests from around the world. It was a place where he had surrounded himself with memories, conversations and shared moments with old friends, new friends and dignitaries alike. With that, Madiba stepped out into the fresh morning air of Houghton, Johannesburg, never to return.

Madiba did not "go gentle into that good night". In his life-time, he was the baby from Mvezo, the young boy from Qunu, the teenager from Mqhekezweni, the student from Herald Town, Alice and Idutywa. He became the young man from Sophiatown and was exiled in middle-age from Soweto to Robben Island. As a grandfather, he returned to Pretoria and took up the seat of power as President. In the autumn of his life, he returned as a great-grandfather to the Eastern Cape. At the close of his life, he lies buried as an elder alongside his family, back where it all began.

In the process of our interaction, he aided a young boy into adulthood. This man, now a legend, taught me that to remain relevant, one must serve. At birth, he was named Rolihlahla, which means to shake the branch of the tree. He certainly shook things up.

The last image I ever took of Madiba is a poor, inferior photo, an underexposed, slightly blurred photograph, taken in haste as Madiba passed me. As we waved goodbye, I was unaware that my time with Mandela had come to an end.

So, there it is, expressed perhaps a little inadequately, but laid down nonetheless. It began as the story of a young boy who had a dream to one day shake the hand of Nelson Mandela. To reach that goal, he spent ten years writing letters or simply sitting outside buildings where Nelson Mandela was present, in an attempt to shake his hand.

In the end, I received so much more than a handshake. I made a commitment that would one day save and transform my life, and bring me the hope and inspiration I needed to become someone. In my journey to Mandela, as in a lesser journey to find a rock where two actors once re-enacted our troubled past, I discovered that it is the journey, rather than the end result, that matters. Having a dream and pursuing the highest ideals of a long-held goal often supersedes the goal itself. That is what gave me a life worth living.

The dream to one day shake the hand of Nelson Mandela held me on course during life's storms. It determined my choices and prevented me from making a number of decisions which had the potential to ruin my life. It was a dream, as unimaginable as it sounds, that held my whole life together.

Never let anyone tell you that a dream requires the right conditions or a specific place and time to begin. It begins from within, because hope springs from within us, and as long as hope is alive, that fire will burn and never die.

"The Light shines in the darkness, and the darkness has not overcome it."   **- John 1:5, NIV Bible**

ACKNOWLEDGEMENTS

This book began on a flight from New York back to Johannesburg. I hadn't considered writing a book before then, but during that flight it all came together. I began the flight talking with an American missionary heading out to Africa for the first time. We shared a few stories and it was in that moment that I realised I needed to write a book. Right there and then I began to sketch an outline of potential chapters on the back of the airline 'sick bag'. For sixteen hours, throughout the night, somewhere over the Atlantic Ocean, the pieces came together under a single overhead light glowing in the economy class cabin. It was as if the whole story was there in my mind already, waiting to be brought to life. Even now, when I hold this book I'm amazed at how many of the stories pieced together here, have shaped what I still consider 'an ordinary life'.

By the time we landed in Johannesburg, I had the bones of what I felt might perhaps work as a book. I had created other books, but those are photographic books, containing large images and minimal writing. Now I wanted to use words to take readers deeper into the lives of the people and places behind the images. Once I got my mind around the fact that I was a photographer writing a book without images, the rest fell into place.

When I take a step back to appreciate the complexity of how

so many of these stories came about, I'm mindful of the bigger picture and the influence of both those who do and don't appear in this book. It's all quite staggering.

The older I become, the more I appreciate the importance of family. To my brother, sisters, moms and dad, I am so grateful to have you all in my life –thank you.

I was only 24 years old when I first stepped through the doors of the Nelson Mandela Foundation offices. What I thought would be a once-off experience turned into an ongoing relationship. The seeds of that relationship were sown approximately nine years before my first visit to the Foundation, when I began writing, asking, begging and even pleading for the opportunity to meet 'Madiba'. The Nelson Mandela Foundation office is a place I have loved going to. It was where I found a home amongst the daily happenings surrounding Mandela's life. For me, it became inconsequential whether Mandela was in the building or not; I loved being there, soaking up everything that was going on. I have a deep respect for everyone I had the privilege of working with at the Foundation. Even when I landed myself in trouble, whilst being reprimanded, I'd sit there admiring the commitment and dedication you all had to promoting and protecting the phenomenal legacy of Nelson Mandela. Thank you, Verne Harris; you believed in me throughout the last 10 years of Madiba's life and even today we continue our friendship. Your influence and belief in me continues to inspire and motivate the work I do.

Over the past twenty years, my progression and maturity as a photographer has been given wings by a host of organisations, institutions, foundations and companies who believed in my ability and skill to translate their stories into images. I am immensely proud to have had the privilege of serving your causes.

My respect and thanks to:

The Nelson Mandela Foundation, the Vodacom Foundation, the Desmond Tutu HIV Foundation, The FW de Klerk Foundation, Oxfam International, the National Underground Railroad Freedom Center, the World Health Organisation, the European Commission, AngliCORD (Anglican Overseas Aid), Australian Volunteers International, the Apartheid Museum, the Annie Lennox Foundation, AusAID, UNAC, MONASO, the SA National Archives and Heraldry, the Wilderness Foundation, Save the Children (SA), Trialogue, Kearsney College, the MW Arts Trust, One Young World, the Hillcrest AIDS Centre and Woza Moya Trust, Vukukhanye, DEG Bank, the Robben Island Museum, the Palace of Justice (Pretoria), Investec, the Ewing Trust, the Vienna State Ballet, the Royal Opera House, the Royal Ballet School, the Cincinnati Ballet, and the Cork City Ballet.

Thank you:

Thomas More College, Sarnia Primary School, Bethany Convent, the Mandela family, Verne Harris, Zelda la Grange, Ahmed Kathrada, Denis Goldberg, Winnie Madikizela-Mandela, Jack Swart, Sello Hatang, Buyi Sishuba, Molly Loate, Helen Suzman, Chief Mangosuthu Buthelezi, Pieter Dirk Uys, Aubrey and Gwen Mokoape, Kenneth Kaunda, Richard and Sharon de Klerk, Sean and Kate Charteris, Deborah Cowley, Lindsay Shmauss (Houghton), Guy Crosbie, Briony and Mike Bosse, the Telfer family, the Parker family, the Arnsater family, the de Klerk family, Moira and John Wild, St Agnes Church, my cell group, the Hall family, the Hermès family (Paris), Karen Moshal, Leigh Erwin, Michelle Gray, Candice Garbin (Hodder), Carolyn Perret (Mackintosh), the Hamilton family (Tzaneen), Tessa Rayner,

Travis Cottrell, Jonathan Orton (assistant editor), Max and Wayne Fowles (FotoMAX), Jonathan Shapiro, Paul Weinberg, Gille de Vlieg, Dawne Oosthuizen, The Rod and Tripod, Neil and Lynley Watson, Zofia Gooch, the Gooch family, Nolucky and Zuko Nxasana, the Mavundla family, Richard Wallis, Antonio Coppola, Brad Thompson, Barbara Botha, Sue McMahon, Catherine Pendock, Borre Sordahl, Les and Hazel Stanley, Jill Drummond, John and Francie Pepper, Richard Cooper, Adam Parker, Alan Foley, Mark and Melda Lansdell, Manfred Jacobs, Ntsika Dlamini, Alan Foley, Malcolm Lyle, Dawn Haynes, Fée Halsted, Di Gain, Paula Thomson, Tom Bartley, Deryck Willans, Dingaan Mahlasela, Victor Wait, Dave Hewett, Richard Wallis, Rae Griesel, Rodney Frank, Harry Wiggett, Kelley Swanby, Lou Harvey, Craig Coombe, Adriaan Diedericks.

To the team at Reach Publishers with special thanks to Lodewyk Bieldt (Book design) and editor Kevin Turner (project editor)

A few special thanks to:

To Annie Lennox: you, my friend, are an incredibly beautiful soul. Thank you for your strength, your music and friendship. I love our times together, your ability to open up space for good conversation, and for always being willing to share, laugh and listen to my stories.

To Archbishop Desmond Tutu: you were the first to extend a hand of support to me, all those years ago. To Lavinia Crawford-Brown, personal assistant to Archbishop Desmond Tutu: you are to be applauded for your dedication and commitment in walking alongside 'The Arch' for so many years. I celebrate you both.

To President FW de Klerk and his personal assistant Brenda Steyn, for your time and unwavering belief in my work. You supported me in my studies, you granted me your precious time for interviews, and allowed me to create images that in years to come will stand as a testament to your courage and vision for South Africa.

A special thank you to Karen Piro for your unwavering support through all the years. I am sure you already know my love and respect for you. You have given me so much over so many years.

To all the dancers out there whom I have had the privilege of photographing: I am in awe of all of you. You are beautiful men and women who gave me the vision of beauty through your amazing ability and sheer talent. I can never say thank you enough.

So the story continues, with great hope and steadfast determination.

"I find I'm so excited I can barely sit still or hold a thought in my head. I think it's the excitement only a free man can feel, a free man at the start of a long journey, whose conclusion is uncertain. I hope I can make it across the border, I hope to see my friend and shake his hand. I hope the Pacific is as blue as it has been in my dreams ... I hope."

- Morgan Freeman, actor, in the closing scene from the film Shawshank Redemption

Nobel Laurette Polish President Lech Walesa

Chairman of Walt Disney Mr John Pepper (left) and US Ambassador to South Africa Mr Patrick Gaspard (Right)

Cinnamon Airways Sri Lanka

Guard Tower Robben Island

Cyril Ramaphosa

ENews TV Interview Morning after Mandela's passing

Former Mexican President Vicente Fox

Hollywood California

Dalai Llama

Channel 9 TV interview Cincinnati Ohio USA

Home based care workers Ixopo KZN

Julius Malema

Hubert Guerrand Hermes, Paris France

Infront of Airforce One

Nobel Peace Prize Laureate Former President FW De Klerk

Nobel Peace Prize Laureate Wangari Maathai

KiSamburu warriors, Northern Kenya

Mandela's bedroom Victor Verster Prison House

Nelson Mandela 24 march 2011

Nelson Mandela Aug 2009

Nick and Nina Clooney, Ripley USA

Nobel Peace Prize Laureate Archbishop Desmond Tutu

Opera Singer Placido Domingo

Presidents Mandela & US President Bill Clinton

Road Tripping with Annie Lennox

Rural community meeting Gaza Province Mozambique

Shawshank Redemption Snyder Road Butler Ohio USA

Singing at Chateau Marmont Hollywood California

Sir Bob Geldof

Tennis player & coach Boris Bekker

The Reverend Jesse Jackson

United Nations Assembly NYC

Winnie Madikizela Mandela

Zelda la Grange Michaelhouse school KZN

White Lodge, Royal Ballet School, Richmond Park, London

Ahmed Kathrada

Cincinnati Ballet Company dance shoot